Strut

How to Kick Financial ASSets in Sexy Shoes

LISA ELLE

BMgmt, CFP, FCSI, CPCA, CCS

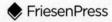

Suite 300 - 990 Fort St
Victoria, BC, V8V 3K2
Canada

www.friesenpress.com

Copyright © 2016 by Lisa Elle (Loewen-Lyttle), BMgmt, CFP, FCSI, CPCA, CCS
First Edition — 2016

Author Photo by Lindsay Nichols Photography

High-heeled boot and strappy sandal graphics by To Uyen from the Noun Project

This book contains the opinions and ideas of its author. It is sold with the understanding that neither the author nor the publisher, through the publication of this book, is engaged in rendering financial, legal, consulting, investment, real estate or other professional advice or services. If the reader requires such advice or services, a competent licenced professional should be consulted. The strategies outlined in this book, including forecast financial information, may not be suitable for every individual and should not be considered as advice or as a recommendation to investors or potential investors in relation to holding, purchasing or selling securities or other financial products or instruments and does not take into account your particular investment objectives, financial situation or needs. The advice and recommendations in this book are not guaranteed or warranted to produce any particular results. All securities and financial products involve risk, which include (but are not limited to) the risk of adverse or unanticipated market, financial or political developments, and in international transactions, currency risk. No warranty is made with respect to the accuracy or completeness of the information contained herein. Both the author and publisher specifically disclaim any responsibility for any liability, loss, or risk, personal or otherwise, which is incurred as a consequence, directly or indirectly, of the use and application of any of the contents of this book.

ISBN
978-1-4602-8822-1 (Hardcover)
978-1-4602-8823-8 (Paperback)
978-1-4602-8824-5 (eBook)

1. BUSINESS & ECONOMICS, PERSONAL FINANCE
2. SELF-HELP, PERSONAL GROWTH, SUCCESS

Distributed to the trade by The Ingram Book Company

You have brains in your head. You have feet
in your shoes. You can steer yourself in any
direction you choose. You're on your own.
And you know what you know. And YOU
are the [gal] who'll decide where to go.

—Dr. Seuss

To my Sweet D's:

Share *love* and *serve* your world with *relentless passion.*

—xoxo

To my Shoes en Blanc Girls:

Thank you for showing up in my life, and for consuming copious amounts of wine in your efforts to help me write this book. Thank you for laughing and crying with me both when I stumble and when I *strut.*

—xoxo

THE SHOE CLOSET

OUTSOLE: PREFACE

Confession: I have more than 150 pairs of shoes. Don't worry—these aren't the $300–500 per pair variety. I am not the Carrie Bradshaw of the financial planning industry. The most I spend on a pair of shoes typically is $20. If I'm feeling particularly impulsive, I may go on a crazy splurge and spend $35.99.

I'm convinced the shoe gods at the Ross Dress for Less chain stores in the US intentionally use those gooey, ultra-sticky price tags so they feel justified in selling a $90 pair of shoes for $13.99. I have few pet peeves in my life, but those tags are at the top of my list. One would think with all the technological advancements of our age, by now someone would have created an easily removable price sticker that doesn't leave a residue.

To add insult to injury, after picking at the goo for twenty-five minutes, it still remains—a permanent stamp of my thriftiness and inability to exercise self-control when confronted with an affordable pair of stacked heels. I could just leave it there, but then that would get the better of my perfectionist tendencies. Subsequently, all my friends can see that I've spent just $14 on my latest pair of Nine West pumps, which will make them either (a) think I'm cheap, or (b) insanely jealous. So really, by removing the tags, I'm doing *everyone* a favour.

You're probably wondering how I can compare financial planning to those tags. Like it or not, most of the time your financial success is a nagging detail in your life you need to spend time with in order to take care of it—and until you do, it's not going away.

So this conundrum leaves us here, in the midst of my shoe closet, with lots of promise yet no sense of what to wear or where to go. You're not alone; financial planning can be confusing. My goal is to bring *clarity* to you and your money.

The shoe closet: a woman's final frontier. It is the place where many of us find solace, solidarity, and sanctuary. Opening the doors, drawers, or shoeboxes unveils the perfect pair of shoes that your feet are throbbing to get into—or perhaps they are throbbing just thinking about them. Whether the hunt took weeks or you happened to stumble upon the perfect pair, there's simply nothing like finding the shoes you desire.

New shoes are always a fresh start, a blank slate. The moment your manicured toes (or not—I won't judge) slip into those brand new red stilettos, your ordinary feet turn into something magical and beautiful. You took the time to put on something beautiful and to love, respect, and nurture your feet. You stand up and admire how much longer and elegant your legs look, suddenly understanding how Angelina Jolie can make working the red carpet in a five-inch heel look so easy. They practically *breathe* confidence into you.

Maybe the new shoes sat in your closet for years collecting dust, or perhaps you just bought them a mere minute ago and couldn't wait another second to slip your feet into them. No matter the scenario, the feeling of putting them on can be compared only to the sensation of chocolate on your lips. The soles of those beauties don't even have a scratch yet. Part of you internally screams that you don't want to wreck that perfect, unblemished surface, but although you don't yet know the places these new shoes will go, you understand they will become a part of your journey—and ultimately, a part of your story.

Your shoes are often there with you in life's greatest joys and biggest challenges. They see your dirty laundry. They take you to explore and sightsee on a dream trip. They usher your family into the house the day you bring your new baby home from the hospital, and conversely, they tap nervously on the floor of the examining room as you await the results from your doctor confirming that you're not as healthy as you once were. They excitedly brush the foot of your true love the first time you go out or rush you along to meet your loved one at the airport after a long journey away from each other. They move you across the stage or down the aisle, up a mountain, or along a racecourse. Maybe they even give you terrible blisters—a worthy sacrifice, because they just *look so good.*

Whether you love the excitement of finding a fantastic new pair of shoes and have 200 of them or you view the one pair you have as merely a necessity, shoes are woven into your story. You chose them for a reason—be it purely aesthetics or for practical purposes—and they are on your feet during both the pivotal moments as well as the seemingly mundane.

You may be wondering: *what inspired this book?*

You mean besides the fact I am a financial mess sometimes, too? Oh—you didn't know? To be honest, I will never sit here and say I've got it all together. Life isn't built that way; we don't live in that world! Things change too much. And we don't have control of it anyways, so why sweat it?

Financial success is also not about how smart you are or the fact you can do math. Everyone can do math—my child in Grade 2 knows four is less than five. How about the fact that you need to spend less than you earn? Everybody "knows" that, but *doing* it is something completely different.

So here's my story—or rather, the start of how this book came to be.

It was Christmas 2010. We stayed at home for the holidays that year because it was my husband's turn in the family rotation. We were happily married with two small children, and we had just moved into a beautiful new home with a large lot just outside of town. We had two newer vehicles in our driveway, we had new furniture, we had money in our bank account, we had just gotten back from our very classy trip to Maui, and we had five rental properties as well. My husband and I each had our own businesses (his successful, mine not), and I had just turned thirty. I had everything a girl could dream of; in fact, I *did* have everything I dreamed of. I was content, I was happy, but amongst happiness, I was completely frustrated.

This frustration led me to a state of *cognitiva recessus toros*, which is Latin for "lazy ass on couch by choice." It is a word I completely invented (Latin makes everything sound important and real) and just pulled out of my ass (yes, the one that's sitting and growing on the couch). I spent two weeks on the living room couch eating chips and Christmas chocolates while my kids played around me. I read five books in those two weeks—which, by the way, is a *lot* for me, the non-reader, C+ student. I was on a quest, but I didn't even know it yet. I just knew I needed to figure this stuff out, because I felt I had completed my checklist—you know, the one a vast amount of us have been raised to complete: get married and have 2.348 kids, a dog, and own your own home with a white picket fence, blah, blah, blah. It was a wonderful place of comfort. So comfortable, in fact, I felt my ass getting bigger with every Christmas chocolate I ate—not to mention the chips, leftover turkey, and the odd pint of ice cream. I was reflecting on my previous ten years to see if I wanted to do my next ten years differently. Although I had a wonderful family and life, I really needed to find my purpose.

When I was about eighteen years old, I wanted to be a financial planner. I became extremely interested in the stock market, as well as a boy. My wonderful boyfriend at the time introduced me to my then-financial planner, and when I invested back then, I knew for *certain* I wanted to be a financial planner.

I started my own business in 2001, when I got licensed for life insurance sales. I was just finishing my marketing and management diploma at Mount Royal University, and I was working for WestJet, a fabulous Canadian airline, at the time. I was twenty-one, and I was already dating my would-be husband. I continued to get my mutual funds license as well as my accident and sickness license.

Strut

I got married in 2005, the same year I completed my Certified Financial Planning designation—which, by the way, was the hardest exam I ever had to write in my life, and I have great appreciation for my fellow colleagues, as well as anyone with high levels of academic achievement. I was shocked I passed on my first attempt! You need to know now that I am a B student at best (okay, that's a lie—I already mentioned I was a C+ student ... you gotta stop calling me out on this stuff!), not to mention I got a D+ in College Beginner's English 101. I begged my professor to pass me. So naturally this makes me the perfect candidate to write a book... Yes, I'm the one who will write this book like I'm writing a text to my best friend, so bear with me, and keep in mind that's why God created fabulous editors! Thank you to that small army of literary experts!

I continued on to complete my Certified Professional on Aging designation and finish my Bachelor of Management correspondence, which I did very slowly, starting in 2006 and graduating in 2013. I did it while I had two babies at home. I remember my business statistics course was completed from eight to ten o'clock every morning while in my bed with two toddlers watching *Treehouse*. Yes, let's have another cheer for children's TV programming, which I have used as a babysitter on many occasions, and I'm really not ashamed. You gotta do what you gotta do—any parent knows that.

This leads me back to my "lazy ass on couch" days. I felt I was missing my passion and what I was meant to do in this world. I know we all have the music in us for something, and I felt I needed to make my mark in the world and create a platform for what I believed—not just around money, but in life in general, the total scope of what this is all about. For me, financial planning, which is really life planning, is my passion and my special gift—you know, the one you are called upon by something greater than yourself to share with the world. I wanted to write a book to share my mistakes and my passion with you through my lessons, experiences with others, and my education on different topics. But above all, I feel women put such a burden on themselves to be super amazing—which we already are.

These are my own personal demons. Dealing with them is never fun. I felt having kids was not good enough, nor was staying at home, when it is. I felt having a career and earning money was not good enough, when it is. I felt my house was too messy or not good enough, when it is. I want you to be okay with where you are in your life today and with all the craziness that is sitting around you. Life is messy. I want you to sit in your mess and be okay with it. It took me years (and counting) to be okay with sitting in my mess. I want you to sit in your financial mess and be okay with it. I want you to sit in your *relationship* mess and be okay with it. It is what it is, and it isn't what it isn't! I think you need to have that conversation with yourself first.

Have mercy on yourself, love yourself, and please forgive yourself, because as women of any age, this is the hardest thing for us to do. I speak from personal experience. And after we are in a place of gratitude, then I want us to throw on our favourite pair of shoes, go out, and take on the world through sharing. I want to share with you not only this book, but I also want to meet you and hear your story; I want to have you connecting with other women in your community, empowering each other around the conversation of life planning. As Arianna Huffington puts it very well in her book of the same name, I want you to "thrive."[1]

This book is my voice, along with a sprinkling of lots of other voices that have informed my life in one way or another. Nothing is original about this book; financial stuff has been around forever, and if not forever, then the CRA just sent it out in a tax bulletin last week—either way, it's the same old stuff.

I am so average, it's not even funny. I tell you this so you can know me as a real woman living a real fantastic, messy, imperfect-yet-perfect life. I pluck the nasty dark hair off my chin every morning and also while at stoplights in my sports car (very sexy!). I laser my moustache at least once a month, and I sometimes break out like I'm in eighth grade. I have stretch marks all over my stomach my two wonderful little girls gave me, and I haven't found a place on my body where cellulite has not moved in and made its home (I keep sending them eviction notices, but the damn cells just don't listen). I topped the scales at 250 pounds—okay, I was 255 pounds on the last

---

1   Arianna Huffington, *Thrive: The Third Metric to Redefining Success and Creating a Life of Well-Being, Wisdom, and Wonder* (New York: Harmony Books, 2014).

day of my pregnancy with my second daughter—and I have been 160 pounds and everywhere in between ... that's a 100-pound difference, and I walked that journey up and down. I've also come to terms with the fact my thighs will touch no matter what size I am. Also, my two beautiful sisters say that my hair needs work, as it looks unhealthy (I have horse hair—and the pictures to prove it). But, again, I'm okay with it, and I embrace the body and looks God gave me, and I work with it.

I'm not perfect, and I love my non-perfection because in it I can relate to women everywhere. For that, I say thank you, dark nasty hairs on my chin. You've humbled me. My point is, the truth is best lived when you can love yourself presently, because you can't share what you don't have. This goes for money, too!

My latest form for discipline with my daughters (ages five and six) has been saying that something's on the line when they act out. For example, if they really want to go to a birthday party and are whining in Wal-Mart (because, heaven forbid any parent takes a well-behaved child into a shopping centre!), I simply say, "Hey, missy, you got a birthday party on the line here if you don't smarten up!" And they do, because usually—not all the time, but usually—they want something so bad their actions and behaviour will alter to get what they want.

I was thinking about this for me. What do I have on the line? What could Mother Marg (Hi, Mom!) say to me when I'm not fulfilling my purpose and living in the way that has my actions and behaviours consistent with the results I want in life? I can honestly say that for my whole life, I've had nothing big on the line, and that bothers me.

We all have nothing on the line. At the end of the day, we'll survive until we don't. We are not going to roll over and die; we typically just don't do that as humans. But, we *will* settle for what's average, because it is usually good enough.

As you learn and grow, "good enough" is not good enough after a while. That's my frustration. It's what has taken me three years to discover for myself, and for me, luckily my frustration led me to great coaches, books, resources, trips, and the right people showing up in my life at the right time. And now, I know without a shadow of a doubt what is on the line for me: it's my purpose, it's my *passion*, it's what excites me, it's what makes me feel alive, it's what makes my heart beat in my chest so loudly I have no other choice but to live this way and fulfill this mission. It's where all my goals flow from for every area of my life: my health, my well-being, my children and the example I want to set for them and the guidance I want to be for them, my relationships with family and friends, my intimate relationships, travel, music, and fun parties. Absolutely everything around me that I create stems from my purpose and flows from what I have on the line.

I found what's on the line for me, and instead of me missing out on a birthday party if I don't smarten up, I'll be missing out on life. I won't be able to share my special and unique gifts with the world—and I know our world is a much better place when we all can share our unique gifts with it.

This sharing requires a community. Because of this, I want you to be a part of my community, sharing your gift while I share mine, creating a better world for us while we are here and for generations to come.

So what's on the *bottom* line for me? Here it is:

Educating women to make empowering financial decisions that will help them create powerful communities around them, resulting in a life that's loved and lived. I want you to find your financial strength.

That's it: I want you to get it and live it, and I won't stop until you do. I finally took all the knowledge (years and years of it) in my head and connected it to my heart, and now here to share my unique gifts in an effort to help you explore, challenge, and ultimately find your financial strength.

I think it's important we define "wealth" before we get started. When dealing with financial planning and finances and money in our daily lives, we need to be clear on our ultimate objectives. One of my financial textbooks said it best:

> What is the objective of wealth management? In short: happiness. But happiness is too imprecise a concept to work with, and wealth alone is not enough to guarantee happiness. All the same, everyone needs some degree of wealth or income to survive. Acquiring and preserving wealth is, after all, a major part of most people's lives and concerns. Wealth is not the end, however; it is one of the means of ensuring happiness. The nineteenth-century political economist and philosopher John Stuart Mill expounded the idea that maximizing human happiness, or utilitarianism, was the proper objective of a person's life. In economics and finance research, this has been translated into maximizing the utility of wealth. Along the way, the overall problem of maximizing utility of wealth turned into maximizing utility of specific parts of a person's wealth, independent of other parts.[2]

Our society has done just that. It has turned the wealth of happiness, self-expression, and fulfillment into dollar signs and net worth statements—they are tools, and yes, money does help you buy food, but they are not the true measure of a person, nor are they *you*. I don't want you to identify yourself with your net worth, or with the mistakes you've made along the way. You are you; you are not your failures.

My goal with my clients, my practice, and this book is to help you find your wealth without numbers while also remaining cognizant of the financial matters that do play into your day-to-day life. Therein lies the balancing act.

It has taken me fifteen years to get to this. I'm a slow learner, and I adapted this from Tim Minchin, who said in his 2013 UWA

---

2 "Chapter Two, Personal Risk Management," *Advanced Retirement Management Strategies*, page 2.7, published 2014 by CSI Global Education, Inc.

address to its graduates: "Life is a shoebox. It is empty and meaning-less—and it's up to you to fill it full and with meaning."[3]

SOLE QUOTE: "Since all great journeys start with a single step, you should probably have on a cute pair of shoes."

3 "Tim Minchin UWA Address 2013," YouTube video, 18:16, posted by The University of Western Australia, October 7, 2013, https://www.youtube.com/watch?v=yoEezZD71sc.

INSOLE: INTRODUCTION

**hat is** it about shoes that make women so excited? I may never fully understand what shoes can do for us, but I know that the right pair can be empowering and can make us feel strong and sexy. Shoes are a fun extension of our personalities.

I'm going to make an obvious confession here: I love shoes! *Love* them. I really just wrote this book as a legitimate reason to deduct my shoes (strictly for research purposes, of course). That's the financial planner side of me: always looking for any possible tax write-off.

However, I also want to have fun with this! And, even if you won't, I will. I know the words "fun" and "financial planning" don't seem to be a natural fit. I can see people's eyes roll into the back of their heads as soon as the topic of personal finance arises. But just as creating the sole of a shoe is the first, basic step when making a shoe, this introduction is my "sole" of the book. I want to make this as meaningful and easy to understand as possible—and what better way to attack such a serious topic than to use a subject that binds so many women together: great shoes?

When you are finished reading this book, I want you to have the confidence to say you can own your personal financial situation. I want you to take strength and satisfaction from that area and then apply it to other areas of your life where you want to succeed in the same way. You have your whole life ahead of you—why not make the most of it?

I am a strong supporter of the shoe industry. As I have mentioned, I personally I have more than 150 pairs! You're probably thinking either "that's really not that many," or "that is completely ludicrous!" I must add a caveat that reveals a much less desirable trait: I tend to hold on to things from the past, so some of those shoes are still from around the time my feet stopped growing in high school. I'm not quite at the hoarder level of keeping old, broken shoes around, but if the pair still fits and looks good, I think it's probably a wise investment to keep it until it comes back into style, even if that means hanging on to it for a few decades. I'll appreciate it when I don't have to re-buy styles I already owned—or, at the very least, my daughters will be extremely grateful when they need a retro costume and suddenly I'm the coolest mom in purple clogs on the block.

I've had a few people tell me I'm crazy to keep all my older shoes around. But shoes tell a story—*my* story. They've been a part of my milestones, or they've marked important events. They've become a part of my identity in a small way. They make me taller, and they give me a different perspective.

When I told a girlfriend I was thinking of writing a nonfiction finance book for women, she thought maybe a theme of "Do as I say, not as I do" would be my best approach. It's true: I have made many financial mistakes. And you know what the strange part is? I'm not ashamed of them. I try to wear them with pride, just like I proudly wear my sexy thong with my fat ass hanging out. So let's get one thing straight: this is not an advice book. Hell no. Please do not show this book to your financial advisors and tell them I told you to go buy 150 pairs of shoes to follow in my footsteps—literally.

Rather, I want this book to be about education and information, with a bit of humour thrown in. Above all, I want it to be about money mercies.

Money mercies, in case you were wondering (and I know you were), is when you arrive at a place where you accept where you are financially, take responsibility for your situation (because you created it), be okay with it, and forgive yourself if you have to. It's at that pivotal moment you decide to set a goal, get off the path you were on, and create a new financial destiny for you and the people you love in this world. That is money mercy, and if you take anything from this book, I hope it's that, while having some fun along the way. And I couldn't think of anything more fun for women of all ages than shoes! Well, maybe Channing Tatum. Okay, definitely Channing Tatum. But he wasn't available, so shoes it is.

When we take responsibility for where we are in life and what we want out of it, the magic begins to happen and a whole new world unfolds for us. Taking responsibility for being exactly where you currently are financially will give you the power to be exactly where you want to be.

Consider this book an opening for conversation. It's not the be-all and end-all of financial books, because no one can write a book about another person's exact financial situation; that is based on your own decisions anyway. This book is meant to empower you to make financial decisions with confidence. I know you may already be aware of many of the things I write about, and I know those reading this will be at varying levels financially and come from a wide range of incomes as well. If I can make this a bit fun and share some good stories along the way and you learn one thing you didn't know before, I'll be ecstatic and consider this project a success. So when reading something you have already heard but could use a reminder of, or something you already know and are currently taking action on, or something you have actually implemented in your life, I encourage you to take the time to acknowledge your success in that. Sometimes we just need reassurance we are on the right track and heading in the right direction.

I want to encourage conversation. One of my greatest joys in life is sharing different perspectives and stories—it's something that excites and fulfills me, so please, speak up and tell me. I promise I'll still like you if we go for coffee to chat and we disagree; in fact, I *want* that to happen! Because that's what this book is: a collection of my ideas and opinions based on my experiences. If one of them adds value to your life, then I've accomplished what I set out to do. I want to be part of the transformation that occurs in the lives of others, even in the smallest of ways, like the way a tiny ripple moves and expands outward.

Terminology: Financial Coach

I'll be your Financial Coach in this book. That means when you lose, I lose. When you win, I win. We both work hard as a team, so we win and lose as a team. But like any good coach, I will push you to achieve the goals you set for yourself. I'm there to train, to instruct, to prompt to action, to teach, to mentor. As your coach, I will seek out answers when I don't know them, and I will be on your side for constant, active guidance and reinforcement. I will also be the person you can call who will talk you off the ledge when you have the overwhelming urge to buy that 151st pair of shoes.

Just because I wrote a book doesn't mean I know all there is to know on these topics, so I'm going to take a stand and insist there's one financial mistake you'll never regret: when faced with a tough decision of any kind, open your mouth and ask for help. There is *no* shame in it. Think about it this way: the richest people on the planet typically have the most help. So ask away! My personal belief is that anything can be accomplished through community.

I was told when writing a book to stick with words I know—but how many people would buy a book with "I," "he," "she," "it," "is," and "unicorn" repeated over and over? All joking aside, just know if you come across a word you've never heard of in the book, take heart—I probably found it on Google.

I chose the shoe theme to make this book as fun as possible, for you and hopefully me as well. Because shoes are with us as we take important steps in our lives, it made sense to use different styles to correspond with the different chapters of our lives. It is my hope to help highlight and shed light on areas you may need to be aware of.

As Socrates says, "an unexamined life is not a life at all."[4] So let's examine these trouble areas, face them with as much gusto as we would a Christian Louboutin sale, and go for it. I'm here to help you overcome the fear surrounding some of these topics that may initially seem overwhelming.

Every chapter is named after a shoe that represents a different financial topic. I could have written a book on each one of these topics, but instead, I offer my best practices as well as advice I have been given and learned in my years as a financial planner. You will also find a few great (and hopefully inspiring) quotes as well as a list of books and resources related to that subject or that will help you grow personally.

Here is what you will find at the end of each chapter:

SHOUT IT OUT is a positive declaration meant for you to speak out loud to yourself daily. However, if you find yourself in the shoe department and have the sudden urge to declare it loudly, go ahead—life is short! Tell people your intentions and how amazing you are.

PUTTIN' ON THE SHOES is a list of action items you can take today or questions you can ask to help yourself clarify where you are in relation to your personal financial goals.

SHOEBOX NOTES is a quick summary of the chapter, highlighting important takeaways. If you wish, you can print these off from my website and then put them in a shoebox, but I recommend keeping a few that have resonated with you in sight so they stick with you.

FAB READS is a list of recommended books to help you on your journey. I've read them all, and each one has value and information that has helped me. Keep these out to use and read; don't shove them in the corner of your shoe

---

4   Socrates, quoted in Plato, *Apology*, trans. Benjamin Jowett, *The Internet Classics Archive*, Massachusetts Institute of Technology, http://classics.mit.edu/Plato/apology.html.

closet with your loafers from the '90s. They will benefit you best if they're out on your nightstand, highlighted, dog-eared, and worn from use.

To mix it up, at the end of each chapter I also include one **FUN SHOE FACT**, a **SOLE QUOTE** (quotes about shoes), and a **SOUL QUOTE** (quotes about life I've personally fallen in love with—and also because all those hours I've spent pinning inspiring quotes on Pinterest are finally paying off).

And because everything comes to life with music—writing, reading, and movies—and music stirs the soul, at the very end of every chapter are **STRUT TUNES**. All these songs have something to do with shoes, boots, walking, dancing, or stepping, and all of them are meant to encourage you to strut your stuff. It's such a crazy mix of music—don't worry: I don't expect you to like them all. I include a bit of every genre to spice it up. You can listen to them while reading that chapter or just listen to them for fun.

I invite you to discover for yourself the amazing possibility you are in the world when you take on an area of your life and pursue it to the best of your ability. I want to help you through these pages, and together—along with some paper and a pencil—I will guide you on your financial track.

This book will help you navigate your financial world with confidence, and it is my hope this will pour out into other areas of your life, and you will *strut*. So stand tall or sit up straight, look in the mirror, and dream of the moments you will have with these shoes—the events they will see and the places they will take you. Then you must take your first step....

1

Slippers

We wake. Sometimes, with no thought to our day, and without realization, we slip—slip into comfort, and not dare to put on the shoes that will lead us out of the house. Magic happens outside our comfort zone.

STYLE DESCRIPTION: A comfortable, slip-on shoe that is worn indoors.

PROSPERITY DESCRIPTION: Comfort is a strange illusion that makes us believe we are in control, and it steals us away from our own personal greatness.

Oh **mornings,** how I've fallen in love with them! I just want to sit here and puke happy morning sunshine all over you. But don't worry, I won't—mostly in the interest of self-preservation, as I know a few night owls, and they're scary before what they consider an acceptable waking time.

However, for me, the possibilities of a new day put the biggest smile on my face. I'll add the caveat this optimism is only a reality with the assistance of coffee. And if I run out of cream ... it's not pretty.

Whether you're in the early-morning camp or not, you still have to wake up at some point, and this actually goes hand in hand with financial planning (well, planning in general).

Your morning, defined as simply as possible, is whatever time you wake up. I'm not going to put a box around it for you (again, I value my life too much). It's simply the first one-to-three hours of your day, whenever that may be for you. For me, the best mornings start around 4:30 or 5:00 a.m., when I experience that magical hour before the rest of the world (namely, my kids) gets up—or at least that's what I tell myself. These initial, daily dialogues you have with yourself provide a time for you to program your attitude and plan your day. These are known as your "hours of power," a.k.a your "power hours."

Mornings took on a whole new meaning for me when I read Laura Vanderkam's book *What the Most Successful People Do Before Breakfast.*[5] It's absolutely fascinating what the most successful, game-changing people on this planet do with their first few hours of the day. After conducting interviews, Vanderkam observed successful people have the most control of their schedules first thing in the morning; this is when their purposes and passions are clearly defined, and they know later in the day other people's priorities take over their own. *Forbes* did a similar study. It was revealed most CEOs are awake before 6:00 a.m. every day. While many of us are only ever going to be CEOs of our wine racks, I think it is *so* important just

---

5 Laura Vanderkam, *What the Most Successful People Do Before Breakfast: And Two Other Short Guides to Achieving More at Work and at Home* (New York: Portfolio, 2013).

to calm and quiet your mind in whatever fashion—through prayer, meditation, yoga, reading, writing, running, or whatever works for you—before the craziness of your day begins. I think it helps us to remind ourselves to keep the main thing the *main thing*, and not get caught up in the stuff of life that just doesn't matter at the end of the day.

I was in a serious slump last year and had to reengineer my days because they just weren't working for me. I was acting without integrity, and I wasn't being true to myself. That's one of the worst feelings. Your whole life seems to fall apart when you aren't acting true to yourself. Women know this best; we will be true to our families, friends, and work, always leaving ourselves until the end, and it's not healthy.

> "Be nice to yourself. It's hard to be happy when someone is mean to you all the time." —Christine Arylo[6]

So I decided to love myself, and start living that way. And surprise, surprise, when you do that, you are more vibrant and alive, and that energy and vitality start to seep into other areas of your life.

Then one night, I came up with a list of three things—three *little* things that control all the *big, important* things—that I find need to happen for me to have killer power hours every day. Marie Forleo, my guru and business coach, refers to them as "non-negotiables." I love that term. These are the things that are so important that if the first few hours of my day are successful, then the rest of the day can go to hell in a hand basket, and I don't feel like I'm behind the eight ball of life. And that, my friends, is the best feeling. Who wants to feel like they are always frantically trying to catch up?

It's like any compound interest account. Preparing in the mornings and setting the key decisions for your day will lead you to a great day, which will turn into weeks, then months, then years, and ultimately, an amazing, well-lived life. Making the decision before

---

6 Christina Arylo, quoted in *Tiny Buddha: Simple Wisdom for Complex Lives*, accessed January 16, 2016, http://tinybuddha.com/wisdom-author/christine-arylo/.

bed that you will have a productive morning will in fact shape your days and help transform your life into what you are looking for.

Your non-negotiables may look very different from mine. Find inspiration from books, blogs, and websites to craft your ideal morning. Above all, keep it realistic. For example, your ideal morning plan should not include waking up every day next to Channing Tatum. I would know—this was in my first draft. Here's what my final (rational) one looks like, which I've called my "Big-Three-For-Life":

1. **Every night before bed, plan out the next day**. Write it out with pen and paper. Consult online calendars, or put it in your phone—whatever. But it's a well-known fact if you write it out and put it somewhere visible to you, it sticks with you and is harder to avoid.

Also, if you write out any dilemmas or problems before bed, typically your subconscious mind will go right to work on finding the solution. Before bed, you can also ask your subconscious to solve a problem. If you are spiritual, pray for it. Have a small bit of faith the answers you seek will come to you, and they will. This will keep you on track for the next day and give your day purpose.

Even if your plan for the day entails day drinking in your pyjamas while watching *The Real Housewives Have Toddlers in Tiaras Because They Didn't Know They Were Pregnant and Now Have Nineteen Kids and Counting*, it will be planned and intentional. This will avoid the issue of finding yourself drifting and having unproductive days that make you collapse because you are defeated from doing nothing. Trust me. I have my eight morning habits I swear by (although in all fairness, three of them are simply "Drink another cup of coffee"). When you live with purpose, it reenergizes you, fills you, produces feelings of happiness and accomplishment, and revolutionizes your life, whatever your purpose may be.

2. **Lay out the appropriate materials to give yourself a successful morning**. This means, if you plan to work out at 5:00 a.m. (don't laugh; some people really do that), have your alarm set for a half-hour earlier, and lay out your runners, workout clothes (sleep in them if you have to), water bottle, and headphones, and have your iPhone or other musical device charged.

If you want to write, put out your pen, notebook, iPad, or laptop, and prep your coffee pot the night before.

Try it with your kids, too. Have them set out their clothing, breakfast, and lunch, and put their packed backpacks at the door ready to go (or do this for them if necessary—there's nothing worse than trying to find matching socks for your three-year-old as you're trying to run out the door). This will make your mornings run more smoothly for the most part. Even on the mornings that *don't* go as planned, you won't feel as though you're left totally scrambling, which would give you the opportunity to forget or miss something important.

This is why the most successful people in the world wake up early. Those two quiet hours—where there are few demands of emails or phone calls or children—are precious. If you start waking early, you may even be able to start the day off really well with a bit of morning delight (if you catch my drift). Most of the men I know won't even complain about being woken up at an unholy hour for that purpose.

This is the time your creative genius is unleashed; this is your time for exercise, meditation, prayer, learning, and writing.

3. And finally, there is **practice positivity and creating intention.** These are declarations. Make sure to plan out your word power for your morning, and say it before you go to bed. Maybe even write it out again every day to really reinforce it. Word power statements may include:

- A personal mission statement
- Goals
- Verses and quotes
- Scriptures
- Uplifting books
- Books on tape
- TED talks
- MarieTV (my favourite every Tuesday!)

Strut

⌐ Anything where you can take five minutes to get inspired by something helps to reinforce your purpose and create possibility in your day

Listen to this, read it out loud, write it, live it, breathe it—whatever works to empower you. Even the Bible says how powerful a spoken word is (Proverbs 18:21), as does Napoleon Hill of *Think and Grow Rich*: "Think twice before you speak, because your words and influence will plant the seed of either success or failure in the mind of another."[7]

Or you can do what I do: buy a dry erase marker and write these power statements on your bathroom mirror, where they'll be the first thing you see in the morning, or on the windshield of your car, where you can meditate on them instead of catching what's happened on Facebook in the five minutes since you last checked, or instead of stressing about that stray chin hair you can actually see now that you're in natural light.

So there it is, my "Big-Three-For-Life." I truly believe a little planning and love go a long way, and the rest naturally falls into place. As John C. Maxwell says: "You cannot enjoy others until you enjoy yourself because you cannot give to others what you do not have."[8]

Don't leave your mornings or power hours to chance, because that sets the tone to leave the *rest* of your day to chance. Prepare to do something creative, rewarding, fulfilling, productive, energizing, rejuvenating, and/or focused. I know from experience it's in these few first hours that, as your internal dialogues wake you up and settle into your head for the day, you are ultimately launching the choices that inspire the kind of life you truly want to live.

Forbes also suggests making your day top-heavy. Get the things you like the least out of the way first to make room for the things you enjoy later in the day. Mornings help shape your attitude for the rest of the day, and your attitude sets you up for success.

---

7 Napoleon Hill, *Read, Think and Grow Rich: All Time Bestseller Reproduced and Updated for the 21st Century*, ed. Veli-Matti Vesikko (public domain, 2016), 1.

8 John C. Maxwell, *25 Ways to Win People: How to Make Others Feel Like a Million Bucks* (Nashville, TN: Nelson Publishers, 2005), 3.

I remember very little from my elementary school years, but my biggest takeaway was from Mr. Satterbloom's Grade 6 class: "Plan your work; work your plan." Thanks, by the way, Mr. Satterbloom! I've used that far more than any "Mad Minute Multiplication" tests. The bottom line is this: power hours and mornings go hand in hand—it's the freshest time of your day.

Shoes for thought: At a conference I once attended, a speaker pointed out how funny it is we put so much focus on sleep. We ask our kids, our partner, our friends, our co-workers the famous morning questions: "How was your night?" or, "How did you sleep?" Immediately, we are forced to reflect on our night in regards to the quality of our sleep, how many hours we got, the baby that woke us up a million times, the dog that got sick, or the snoring that kept us awake.

Why not change the conversations we have in the morning and completely throw people for a loop? We spend so much time worrying about how we (or the people we care about) sleep. Here's the thing: we can sleep when we're dead. Let's talk about the hours we're awake! Why not say something like, "I got eighteen hours of *aliveness* in yesterday!" instead of the traditional, "I got only four hours of sleep last night." What a different conversation we would create about that period of time when life is actually happening.

You're now asking what this has to do with financial planning. Remember, to know where you are going and what you want to accomplish in regards to your goals, your mission, and your passions, you need to focus and reflect on what you're doing in the periods you're awake to help create the opportunities that will make this a reality. Financially speaking, money plays into everything we do; so make sure you know what you want to accomplish, be it a short-term goal or long-term plan. Either way, the money comes behind the "why." Money will never fulfill you—you know that. It's just currency for accomplishing dreams and living life.

Simon Sinek's famous TED talk, "Start with Why," describes just that.9 Everything you do will stem from your "why." You need

9 Simon Sinek, "Start with Why," TED Talk, *TEDx Puget Sound*, September 2009, https://www.ted.com/talks/simon_sinek_how_great_leaders_inspire_action?language=en.

to know your why before you can do any financial planning; otherwise, you are the ship without a rudder, going nowhere fast and spinning in circles. So when you get out of bed and put on your comfy slippers, remember the why: it will centre your day and your life.

I hope you're inspired to enjoy the cozy times of the morning, which will ultimately lead to the shoes of your choice for that day. But it all starts with the slippers....

FUN SHOE FACT: In Hungary, the groom drinks a toast to his bride out of her wedding slipper. This is an interesting way to show your betrothed romantic love, no?

SOLE QUOTE: "They went into my closet looking for skeletons, but thank God, all they found were shoes." —Imelda Marcos

SOUL QUOTE: "I love the smell of possibility in the morning." —Taylor Wells

FAB READS:

- *Today Matter: 12 Daily Practices to Guarantee Tomorrow's Success* by John C. Maxwell
- *What the Most Successful People Do Before Breakfast* by Laura Vanderkam
- *Think and Grow Rich* by Napoleon Hill

SHOUT IT OUT: I am amazing. I create my life.

PUTTIN' ON THE SHOES:

➤ Write down three to ten things you can do in your power hours, and then decide on the non-negotiables that will make a fabulous start to your day – every day!

➤ Write out your goals, declarations, and intentions and then say them out loud with conviction at least twice day—and believe in those words!

➤ Take action!

SHOEBOX NOTES:

➤ Create and define your mornings: renovate them to serve you and set up your day.

➤ Mornings are fresh starts where are all things can be possible.

➤ Set three goals for each day that contribute to your three goals for the week, month, and then year, because a ...

➤ Great morning = great day = great week = great month = great year = great life.

STRUT TUNES:

➤ "Wake Me Up Before You Go-Go" by Wham!

➤ "I'm Gonna Be (500 Miles)" by The Proclaimers

➤ "A Beautiful Morning" The Rascals

➤ "Feeling Good" by Michael Bublé

2

Flip-Flops

Procrastination and indecision will never be your friend—although they sure like to cuddle.

STYLE DESCRIPTION: A light sandal, typically of plastic or rubber, with a thong between the big and second toe.

PROSPERITY DESCRIPTION: Procrastination and indecision are the flapping sound of not fulfilling your purpose.

My **favourite** go-to shoe! Come summertime, it's really the only shoe you need. For me, a successful week is a week one does not need to wear any other kind of footwear. It's nice not to have to think about what shoes to wear sometimes, and the good ol' summertime standby is comfortable and easy to slide on. However, they are not the most supportive footwear. Did you know in 2010 there were 200,000 injuries related to flip-flops in the UK alone? I know ... you probably just snorted your coffee a little bit (people be cray!), and maybe, just maybe, that information made your blood pressure rise a little to the point where you wanted to start a new Facebook group called "MAFF" (Mother's Against Flip-Flops). This is some serious stuff we are talking about. I mean, we are talking at *least* a billion dollars a year in healthcare costs in the UK. I don't even want to find out how many flip-flop injuries are worldwide, especially in those hot countries where they wear sandals all year round. *Geesh*—that's a lot of flippin' injuries! My advice: make sure it's not you.

Like the shoe, most of us have daily "flip-flop injuries," but more so the kind that cause us unnecessary financial injury. Indecision and procrastination are not our friends. Every time we procrastinate, it usually comes with some financial loss. It's true: the most successful people in the world do one thing very well—they make decisions and stick with them. They don't drag out anything. They realize that if it doesn't work out, that's okay, and they will try again, but they don't live in the space where indecision paralyzes the quality of their life. Nothing feels better than making a decision and sticking to it.

You have to go through the mental stuff—such as figuring out your "why"—in order to gain some clarity into your own life and do some self-work before you can truly benefit from how you want your money picture to look.

A few years ago, I went to the Calgary Stampede and impulsively decided to wear heels. I looked and felt sexy, which led to that decision—albeit in hindsight, it may not have been the brightest decision I've ever made. But that's okay; the painful blisters just forced me to rethink my footwear for the next two days. Remember:

the beautiful thing about our mistakes is that we learn something from them, often about ourselves, and that is what we want, and what we don't want. So I say, the more mistakes we make, the better.

"Remember when you fall on your face, you are still moving forward." —Ron Barbaro

If time is money, then indecision costs a lot. It takes away from your quality of life. This will apply to anything you do. Need to decide what paper to write? Or which way to take your business? What career path to embark on? Which restaurant to go to for dinner? Or which shoes are a better match with that outfit?

With all the decisions we are faced with in a given day, let alone our whole lives, it's no wonder that we waste so much time just deciding whether or not we should go for caramel drizzle on our latte today. Once we decide, however, a sense of peace follows. (Side note: get the caramel. Always get the caramel.) Whether we choose right or wrong, it doesn't matter. It's just better to know where you are going and what you are doing.

The same goes for financial matters. The biggest obstacle that will hinder your financial goals is indecision. Did you buy the wrong investment or choose the wrong stock? At the end of the day, according to Nick Murray, a top advisor to financial advisors, it's not timing the markets that matters, it's time in the markets that matters.[10] So don't be worried if you should have gone with fund A or B or line X or Y; just go with it, and providence will go with you.

When we flip-flop on our intentions and goals, the universe can't support our indecision. Be clear, and just decide—you can change your mind if you need to. Worrying helps nothing, as 95 percent of the things we fret about never come to fruition anyway.

---

10 Nick Murray, "Client's Corner: It's Always About Time, Never About Timing," *Financially Sound Life Planning*, http://financiallysound.ca/wp-content/uploads/2014/03/s-Always-about-Time-not-Timing.pdf.

Comparing Thyself to Thy Neighbour

It happens to so many good people. Blessed are those who don't really care what others think. As a baptized "people pleaser," I know all too well what "comparative-itus" does to me and also what it does to my clients and their financial situations. I'm a firm believer in the anything-is-possible ideology; however, you have to create that opportunity for yourself. I also believe competition solves nothing; there is more than enough to go around. Competition breeds scarcity. We have all the resources in the universe at our disposal, and we have to choose that. Here are a few things to keep in mind about the idea of "normal":

↳ "Normal" exists only because we created it to exist.

↳ "Normal" is just an expectation of being average.

↳ "Normal" is the dangerous place where comforts exist and possibilities dwindle.

↳ We cling to "normal" as if it's a place of safety we use for survival.

And yet we all unconsciously strive for "normal," knowing it really exists only in our heads.

When we try to define normal, we place expectations that it is good enough and some of us even strive for normal or to be part of the "average." However, by staying in normal, we miss out on so many adventures. Normal can be boring. But most importantly, normal doesn't inspire others or create. It can keep us mediocre as we tend to gravitate back to the average, normal. Like my favorite meme says, "the magic happens outside of your comfort zone," outside of the normal.

It's my goal to be bold and to get out of the rut that keeps me trapped in the normal range of existence. So I challenge you right now to do something unreasonable, crazy, or silly. This attitude goes hand in hand with your financial planning. It's all a balance. But whenever you are making any purchase or financial decision, my advice is to just go with it. You may already know the regret of not doing something is far worse than the perceived risk itself.

When I was writing this book, I hosted a research party with twenty-one beautiful ladies, which had absolutely *nothing* to do with drinking wine on a beautiful Sunday afternoon in September. I call them my "Shoes en Blanc" girls, playing on the "Dîner en Blanc" theme. I asked all the women to wear white and their favourite pair of shoes. I booked a beautiful venue I had fallen in love with in the country, and we enjoyed an amazing lunch and a bit (or a lot, but who was keeping track?) of wine.

Then I had the ladies pour out their financial hearts to me. It was fun and fantastic. Not only did I get support and love from my girls that day, but I also got lots of great research and gems of insight I'm so excited to share with you throughout this book—some of it funny, but all of it great.

A few of the ladies had a scale on which to rate items they purchased while shopping. They had what they called a "CPW" system, which stands for "compliments per wear." If you had ten compliments per wear and the item cost you ten dollars, you were batting one thousand. So the more compliments, the more the item purchased was justified. This in turn brought the value of the item up, so something that cost one hundred dollars but got one thousand compliments was virtually free.

They also had one for "WPD"—wear per dollar—so if you bought a ten-dollar item and wore it ten times, your WPD number was one; any item with a WPD of less than one is typically a good buy. So keep in mind when eyeing a pair of Louboutins or Blahniks or Choos, as they will need to be worn a lot to get the WPD down to one. (Economic theories you can share with your husband!)

I find this very important information to share with you. It's economics at its best, and like all things, making good, educated guesses about the WPD of a pair of shoes is the same idea as creating financial projections for yourself. Whether it's a self-fulfilling prophecy or not, typically things do usually go the way they are planned.

Consider this: 99.9 percent of all people without any financial plans at all fail financially. And 65.9 percent of all statistics are made up. Both statements are probably true; you know it intuitively.

We get stuck in the "why" so often in life, and I'm not talking about the "why" of your existence, but rather the "why" of what happens to us. We need to start asking "how," as in, "How can I ...?" That question is where real, significant change begins to occur. Asking "why" probably hasn't gotten you very far.

You are reading this book because there is a part of your financial life that you are not satisfied with right now. And that's perfectly healthy. Healthy people realize this: "There's a gap between what you have accomplished and what you would like to accomplish."[11]

I want to give you the essentials you need to know and help you paint a clear picture in your head of what you want so that you are able to clear out the noise and the useless information. There's just *too much information* coming at us today. Try to remember something that is of value to someone else may be useless to you. Like shoes, financial information is not one-size-fits-all.

There are two things you need to know for any of this book to work or make sense: we need to define "risk" (what the real risks to *you* are), and why you need a financial coach.

First, as I said in my introduction, you need a financial coach sooner rather than later. You need a financial coach (a holistic financial planner or advisor) the same way you need a lawyer, a dentist, and an OB/GYN. Don't ever try to be a do-it-yourself investor. You wouldn't put yourself in the stirrups and try to give yourself a pap smear, right? (Please say right.)

Athletes recognize they need a good coach for their greatest chance at success. However, for some reason, we will hire a fitness coach before we hire a financial one. We also spend more time planning our shoe purchases than we do our finances, but even I'm guilty-as-charged in that regard.

I can't overstate the importance of having your team of people in place, and since you pick the members, you get to make sure it's a winning team. These should be people you can talk to and gain wisdom, advice, and encouragement from. Financial coaches are there to save you from brains that may be hardwired to make bad financial decisions.

11   Nick Murray, *Serious Money: The Art of Marketing Mutual Funds* (Shrewsbury, NJ: R.A. Stanger, 1991), xv.

I'm going to say it one more time: *you need to have a great financial coach on your team* (has it sunk in yet?). You need more than just a service for your insurance or investments that are typical of most banks (yes, I'm not completely opposed to throwing big banks under the bus—it's a love/hate relationship most of the time); I'm talking about someone you can talk frankly to about your *entire* financial picture.

If this is all you get out of this book, it will be worth thousands—if not millions—of dollars to you throughout your life. And for the minimal cost in the big picture, it can save you, your family, your estate, or whatever you are trying to accomplish in your life in a BIG way. Good advice is worth its weight in gold—literally (or your favourite shoes, times one thousand).

I also need to explain in Canada, you will want an advisor who is licensed in both investments and insurance. There are huge financial implications to this. Because the Insurance Companies Act of Canada and the Bank Act of Canada are two totally separate acts, the advisors at your bank will almost *always* overlook very important insurance planning. This is maybe because they aren't informed or trained on insurance and estate matters, or perhaps because it's not what banks specifically sell. They have their bottom lines, too.

You need an independent advisor. There are some who work for banks but typically not at the branch level. This is probably the most unknown of all financial information. For the older generation right now, who have trusted banks for decades, this is a huge disservice to our aging population. This can and will change over time, but for now, it's so important that you find a dual-licensed advisor, one who can cover your insurance and investments or someone who can at least look at your whole picture and send you to the right people to get the products in place that will help you. If you want some help with a cash flow plan, find yourself a Certified Cash Flow Specialist (CCS). They will really help you with the day-to-day management of your money as well.

Getting unbiased advice is an invaluable asset, and I know many great dual-licensed advisors. There is a small army of them in Canada. (I say small because this industry needs more people who care. PERIOD. Want a new career?!)

A great coach is also an accountability partner. A coach will help you measure your success, keep you engaged, keep you connected to your integrity, and help you reach your goals faster than you can doing it alone.

Also, before we create any financial plan, we need to define risk. Without a solid definition, we can't create the proper financial plan to help mitigate potential risks. When you are more specific about your goals, you can better define risk in terms of your planning. There is a lot that goes into risk planning—that is why amongst the most successful businesses in the world, there are insurance companies who do this well. Define risk, measure it, establish a process for managing it, and figure out what is really at risk.

What most financial advisors find funny is that clients are often focused on their rate of return (ROR) or return on investment (ROI), and that is their primary concern. Yet they rarely give much thought to tax planning, which, if invested in the wrong type of account with over contribution, can actually cause you to lose all your gains.

I ask you keep an open mind and remember that all the things we don't know, we don't know. That is why when it comes to investments and planning, having a great coach is so important to shed light on areas that may be overlooked by another professional. After all, we are all just human, and all have our own areas of specialty, so things do get overlooked. This is why having a team composed of your lawyer, accountant, lender, advisor, etc., is such an important thing to get into place for your financial life.

So what is your real risk? Is it you will outlive your money? Is it you won't have enough money saved up to live the life you desire? You'll deplete your current savings due to an unforeseen illness or disability? Those situations are real and legitimate—we hear those stories every day, and we all know someone in one of those situations.

Make sense? Okay, going back to why it is helpful to have a financial planner/advisor/coach on your side, it is also helpful to find an *independent* advisor/planner/coach, which refers to someone who is independent of working for one company that sells one product line and is free to find the best products and services for you, a broker.

Here's why. I need to politely mention you aren't going to be getting your best financial, tax, and estate advice from the walk-in-corner-branch *most* of the time—although banks' marketing departments, along with their billions in advertising, will tell you differently. This is because *banks simply do not offer certain financial products* and therefore cannot offer the financial and tax advice that goes along with it. So I offer up a Starbucks to my banking friends as an apologetic sacrificial offering and pray the next time I walk in to use the ATM I won't be struck down by lightning, or worse—the ATM gods refuse me money.

Now to be fair, I'm actually not really throwing the *big banks* under the bus. The banks have their purpose. However, when we don't keep our minds open to all the financial options available to us, then we are just choosing to live with our heads in the sand (now, if that involves a beach, a book, and no kids—please sign me up!).

This is why your corner bank won't tell you this stuff upfront:

⌐ Perhaps the bank representative you deal with doesn't know these products exist.

⌐ If they do know they exist, they are probably not compensated to direct you elsewhere, or maybe it is a conflict of interest.

⌐ They don't realize the tax or legal implications of your current situation and how other products can help you.

⌐ Perhaps they just don't know because it's not their specific training to be able to identify planning strategies or opportunities.

It's not really their fault; it's just how the system has been set up and running for years. If it ain't broke and makes a few billion every quarter, why change it?

Enter: Independent Financial Advice

A dual-licensed, independent advisor just means this person is able to sell you products (legally and regulated) and is licensed as the following: either IIROC or MFDA licensed and life, accident and sickness insurance licensed.

I'm not going to go into each of the products in detail; the point of my notes below is to bring awareness to financial products that are out there that the majority of the population does not take advantage of.

Here are the **five products** you probably won't be getting from your mainstream banking branch (all of these descriptions have been slightly simplified for clarity):

1 **Corporate Class Mutual Funds**: mutual funds that defer tax to a later date in a non-registered account

2 **T-SWP Mutual Funds**: return of capital mutual funds, tax planning benefits for non-registered money

3 **Segregated Funds**: mutual funds with a life insurance wrapper that have guarantees, offer creditor protection, and bypass probate (estate planning benefits)

4 **Flow-Through Shares**: potential (huge) tax benefits by purchasing flow-through shares of eligible Canadian companies

5 **Life Insurance, Critical Illness, Disability, and Extended Health Insurance**: banks do sell these products through technically another entity; however, if you walk into a branch, legally they can give you a phone number to contact their insurance division. At the time of writing this, you legally cannot buy insurance in a bank branch. You must look elsewhere, even if it's next door to the bank.

I mention all of this because I want you to keep your options open and be able to find the financial products that suit *you* and work with *your* life. Also, having a knowledgeable coach or advisor on your side to help navigate you through the thousands of financial products, funds, investments, insurance products, etc., that are out on the market. Clearly, no advisor will know every product out there, however, most have a good handle on what is out on the market and have sourced out the top products and companies for their best ideas and solutions.

You are hearing it here first: stop flip-flopping. I do have a 6-Week Money Makeover course online that goes through all this planning and gets your footing in place to then take the first steps and get all your money organized on purpose. Check out my 6-Week Money Makeover course at www.ellementsgroup.com!

Side Step: What owns you? Do you know that everything that you purchase ends up owning you? The obvious example is debt, in its various forms; however, I'm saying that *everything* you spend money on has power over your life.

Think of the apple you just bought—the actual fruit, not phone. You have to pay for it, take it home, wash it, refrigerate it, cut it up, maybe bake it (if you want apple pie), eat it, clean the knife and cutting board, throw away the core (unless you are like my grandpa, and just eat the core ... ew! Okay, who am I kidding, I've eaten a live goldfish), and then take the garbage out to the garage and remember to take garbage out on garbage day. All that for one little apple!

Okay, so maybe I'm being a little dramatic, but I want to illustrate how everything we buy ends up owning our time and money. It's not necessarily a bad thing. We need to survive, obviously, and we constantly purchase for emotional reasons. Plus, the enjoyment factor of our possessions is a huge and super important part of life. You have to take care of, fix, repair, service, maintain, clean, and wash whatever it is you buy, from the big purchases (like your home), to the little ones (like your groceries).

The problem occurs when we start to purchase a bunch of crap we don't need. I'm *sure* you've never purchased anything you don't need, and if I walked around your house I wouldn't find anything still with the tag left on it you purchased a while ago.... Yeah, I thought so.

There is only one solution to this problem. Ask yourself this on all future purchases: is it in alignment with your goals and the future you want to create?

If you want to travel the world, maybe owning one vacation property doesn't make sense, and it will keep you tied down. Or maybe your goal is to spend more time with family and friends; in that case, taking a girlfriend out to dinner is a better use of your money than buying your 276th pair of shoes.

If you want to save a million dollars by age fifty, does buying your thirty-fifth purse really bring you closer to your goals?

If something is a drain on your time or resources, maybe it's time to rethink. If your paid-off car is costing you many hours back and forth to the repair shop, maybe it's time for a new car.

More isn't always better; sometimes "more" is just more to deal with that owns your space, your time, and your money. The goods we purchase always have two costs: time and money. Typically it's the "time" part of the cost we don't value properly. Even the free stuff costs our time, at the very least.

"The beauty of minimalism isn't in what it takes away. The beauty and the full potential of minimalism lie in what it gives."
—Joshua Becker

Here's something totally crazy that I have learned lately: *The more crystal-clear you are with your goals (spiritual, health, relationships, family, work, etc.), the more your purchases are in alignment with what serves you and not what takes away from you. You also don't waste money on the stuff you will never eat, wear, or use.*

It's time to do some internal spring-cleaning. Do the hard work! Self-reflect, set your goals, and be transparent about them. (And, yes, goal-setting and knowing what you truly want out of life is hard work—there's no sugar coating it! Most people on this earth don't really know what they want from life, so don't be one of those people. Life will give you what you ask from it.) I promise you that when you have clarity around what you want from life, you won't be spending any money on things you don't need—which is a behaviour that begins the downward spiral of sucking your time and money (my basement full of kids' toys comes to mind). Also, you will notice the areas in which you buy "mindlessly"; those may be the areas in your life you truly don't have defined goals for, or those areas are your problem areas that really need to be addressed in your self-reflection.

For example, my area of struggle or mindless shopping occurs at the grocery store. I have defined goals to lose weight, but I'm a fabulous self-saboteur in this area. I will still sometimes buy chips, chocolate bars, and boatloads of fancy cheeses that totally do *not* serve me or my goals to lose weight. I can walk by almost everything at a mall and not think twice about it, but somehow, I see a display of fancy cheese and I'm totally derailed.

That's something I'm working on. We are all working on some area in our lives; don't assume anyone has it all together. Once we do have it all together then new challenges arise. This is the joy of life!

Bottom line: Do the hard work of goal-setting, because when your goals are set, then alignment will follow easily, your life will move more smoothly in all areas, your bank account will be happier, and money will flow to where it serves you—not to where you are a slave to it. The free man is the man who realizes he owns nothing and is steward over everything that crosses his path.

Side Step: Lottery winners really do tend to squander their wealth in five to seven years, and they often have nothing left to show for it, according to statisticbrain.com and research by Camelot Group PLC in July 2014. I believe this to be true for two reasons: (1) They don't have a plan in place, and (2) statisticsbrain.com says 44 percent of winners spent their entire winnings in less than five years. The point I'm trying to make is to get started on good habits. Start paying yourself first. Many little habits formed over years create amazing success.

In Malcom Gladwell's *The Tipping Point,* he shares how approximately ten thousand hours or ten years in one career begins your taking-off point. The same goes for the little habits you create, and for those starting out. Saving $100 or $200 a month may not seem like that much, but it adds up fast. And if you're going from twenty years old to thirty, trust me, you will be light-years ahead of most other thirty-year-olds. So start young, start old, start these habits at any age. Just start. And when you do win the lottery, call me.

Strut

FUN SHOE FACT: The average American woman owns thirty pairs of shoes, spends an average of $300 on footwear every year, and 60 percent of them regret at least one of their shoe purchases.

SOLE QUOTE: "Shoes are always the most important thing for me because they are who you are. They change the way you walk, the way you move." — Tom Ford

"You cannot act like flip-flops and expect to be treated like Louboutins." — Carrie Bradshaw, *Sex and the City*

SOUL QUOTE: "I seem to be on track in life. I'm just not sure whose track." — Unknown

FAB READS:

- *Eat That Frog!: 21 Great Ways to Stop Procrastination and Get More Done in Less Time* by Brian Tracy
- *The Power of Focus* by Mark Victor Hansen
- *The Strangest Secret* by Earl Nightingale (audiobook)
- *The 7 Habits of Highly Effective People* by Stephen R. Covey

SHOUT IT OUT: I forgive myself.

PUTTIN' ON THE SHOES:

- Fake it 'til you make it (FITYMI): Pretend you already are where you want to be. How would you act? How would you look? How would you live?

➘ Write out your ideal dream day, and then reverse-engineer your dream to discover the steps on how to get there.

➘ Start doing your daily non-negotiables, and create that habit. Also, make sure to follow through and keep your habits aligned for thirty days; otherwise start over (as many times as you need to).

➘ Go to www.ellementsgroup.com/makeover to get started!

SHOEBOX NOTES:

➘ Indecision and procrastination are not your friends.

➘ Don't flip-flop in your intentions; it's the constant tap, tap, tap—like tap shoes—that gets the dance done and will bring about the success you desire. Stay on course!

➘ Make a decision; even one small good financial decision will get you to where you want to go.

➘ Make the decision to have a financial plan, and create one!

➘ Decipher what your real risks are to not living the life you want to live.

➘ Hire a financial coach for your life and money.

➘ Lastly, start living out your passions and plans right now—just start!

STRUT TUNES:

➘ "Send Me on My Way" by Rusted Root

➘ "One Step at a Time" by Jordin Sparks

➘ "Every Little Step" by Bobby Brown

➘ "Shoes" by Tiga

3
Clogs

You are where you are in life because you consented to it—every bit of it. Sometimes you need to say, "I don't consent to this anymore."
—Adapted from William Channing

STYLE DESCRIPTION: A shoe with a thick wooden sole.

PROSPERITY DESCRIPTION: Being weighed down in all sorts of unfruitful things, like debt or negativity, unable to walk swiftly and move forward.

When I say the word "clog," I don't mean that nasty hair clog in your shower that you are too lazy to clean (ewww). I'm talking about good ol' wooden shoe-type clogs; okay, *both* are unpleasant. Clogs, the footwear, have to be the most uncomfortable of all shoes to wear. They are very awkward shoes, not to mention how you really can't run in them; if you do try to run in them, it's more like an eighty-year-old-shuffle-along movement. They were designed to slow you down. Okay, that may not be 100 percent true, but I'm gonna go out on the "common sense" limb and guess that's how it is.

I will never forget my first pair of wooden clogs. I was in seventh grade, and I bought them in Phoenix. They were black wooden platform shoes about two inches thick all the way through, and they had a multicolored top that resembled a Rubik's Cube. They were the coolest shoes at the time, next to Doc Martens, *but* they were absolutely uncomfortable to walk in—as is the debt and financial burdens we carry with us.

This chapter isn't just about financial debt; it's also about the mindsets around debt and how we position our thoughts around money and financial laws: abundance versus scarcity, and creating versus consumption. This chapter is about setting yourself and your mind free.

In case you haven't heard, here is the blurb on debt: there is debt (which is annoying, like a blister on your foot) and there is worse debt (likened to an artery bleeding out uncontrollably).

Is your debt working for you? If not, then get rid of it as fast as you can. (There, that was easy!)

Also, it's important to learn how to run a surplus. You don't need fancy programs or apps to do this. I personally use a sticky note most of the time and jot down what needs to be paid and how much extra there will be. Sometimes simple is best. I love my iPhone, but there are certain things I will still put on paper. Pen to paper is proven to stick better in our minds.

Another way to eliminate our debt is to make more money. Right?! If there is a will, there's a way, and you know that if you truly have the desire to get rid of unsightly debt, you will. End of story: believe you will and you will.

I don't even want to tell you what you already know regarding interest rates and debt. If your investment is earning 8 percent interest and your debt is at a rate of 18 percent, of course you know what you should do. Seriously, we could do that math in Grade 1. (Hint: pay down your debt!) However, I know that paying down your debt is easier said than done.

This is not about math. Math anyone can do. My daughter in Grade 1 can do basic math. This is about balancing what looks good on paper with basic human behaviours. Managing behavioural psychology is going to be the biggest factor in determining your financial success.

So I'm not going to harp on debt this chapter, because I already know you feel guilty about it and want to do something about it. I will tell you the first thing you need to do about it is to forgive yourself for it! You will be able to eliminate debt with a plan, however, you won't be able to change your spending habits without doing the internal work of forgiving and loving yourself.

As a financial coach, my biggest challenge is not about telling you what to invest your money in, or even any of my financial suggestions. It's about getting you to commit to your financial goals— you must commit to your life and to what you want to accomplish with it. If I can keep you from making "stupid" financial mistakes, you will be better off for it, but I can't do that until you commit to your financial goals, and a huge part of that is feeling worthy that you deserve to have money, live an abundant life, and if you choose, be wealthy beyond your wildest dreams!

To start living with an abundant mindset, you need to rule out words like "competition." Competition maybe has its place in sportsmanship and fun but definitely not in business or any other area. There is truly room for each of us to shine and share our uniqueness with the world. As Napoleon Hill reminds us, "The ladder of success is never crowded at the top."[12] Once you truly understand and

---

12 Napoleon Hill, *Read, Think and Grow Rich: All Time Bestseller Reproduced and Updated for the 21st Century*, ed. Veli-Matti Vesikko (public domain, 2016), 2.

believe there is no competition and surrender yourself to that belief, you will begin to live more freely. Scarcity is another deep belief that is rooted pretty strong. There is enough for everyone.

"Value" is a great word. So is "value add"—okay, that's two words, but again, it's not about math. I often think of what my "value add" is in any situation in life. I often keep thinking about how to create value for somebody else. Earle Nightingale, in his audio recording "20 Minutes that Can Change Your Life," talked about how to be of value. He said to be of value, one must create value. He also talked about how the irrefutable law of life is that *your rewards in life are always equal to the value you create—that is, what you put in you get out.*[13] This is a law, like the law of gravity or that of energy, which cannot be created or destroyed. This isn't a man-made law, in which we can sit and debate and form opinions or stories about, but *truth*. We need to understand some of these universal laws, which aren't taught in our traditional educational system. The inquiry into these truths will transform the ways in which you look at the world, and you will begin to see it in play, from the smallest of transactions to the things that rattle your brain due to their seeming incomprehensibility. So to illustrate value and add value, I will use my Shoe Economics story.

I hated economics when I was in college; instead of applying myself, I was usually applying myself with twenty-five-cent draft and anyone I could recruit. Really? You put a bar in a college where eighteen-year-olds could easily rub together a few quarters for trays of draft special, and you proceed to call the establishment "Liberty Lounge"? Liberty won.

I can tell you about supply and demand and economics in general, but although most theories do work (although they are hard to track in their accuracy), you have to realize the game is changing in this minute-to-minute (second-to-second) economy. Although I'm not an economist (because economists probably own only one pair of shoes: penny loafers), the instantaneous market creates the

13   Earl Nightingale, "20 Minutes that Can Change Your Life," YouTube video, 18:49, posted by MartyMcFly1985, August 12, 2013, https://www.youtube.com/watch?v=gYQejJmKbx8.

global economy that we are all part of. We have more ability to track where the funds move, as they are so moving rapidly all around the world, yet too much information to dissect properly most of the time. Breaking down this information into easy-to-understand bites is where the value is.

I love economics now! True story: it totally turns my crank. Give me *Thomas Crown* in a suit any day of the week. I write this from my inaugural trip to New York City, and I'm just in awe of the economics of this big city. There is a certain ebb and flow to business and our global economy. We all have our gifts, and we all play important parts in our economy. Here is a beginner's economics story with the only hopes it will give you some base knowledge to be able to apply it and help you make more informed decisions, and ultimately, not to be so hard on yourself. You heard me right. So much of this is our internal story we tell ourselves, and I want to release you of the guilt you have about money or to your debt. So I will start slowly and with shoe economics. I got most of my ideas from the book *The Richest Man in Babylon*, by George S. Clason. (By the way, it took me a few reads of that book to wrap my head around the "ol' English" style of writing, but after that, it was pure gold.) It's definitely on the must-read list, and I will probably refer to it from time to time in the chapters ahead.

Without further delay, I now welcome you to ...

Shoe Economics 101: An Example of How Wealth Can Be Created

Jimmy Two-Shoes gathers the raw materials needed to make the most beautiful bespoke shoes for you. The resources come from all over the world and contribute to the economies of those places. He gathers:

    $20: leather from Texas
    $10: rubber from Thailand
    $15: synthetic plastic heels from China
    $7: adhesives from India

Jimmy Two-Shoes then creates his masterpiece pair of shoes. He then sells these shoes to you for $1,000 (lucky you—they are one of a kind, you know!).

So is the money you spent on the shoes gone once you take possession of your Cinderella slippers? Has it disappeared? No, a woman in India has some of it and profited off her margin, and so does the gentleman in China—he made a hefty profit on the $15 heels, which cost him $1 to make. As for the young buck in Texas—well, let's just say the steak was so good last night. The elderly lady in Thailand also profited, and Jimmy Two-Shoes got his fair share of $948, as did his company and marketing department. So everyone who laboured on the shoes now has a part. Now that the shoe has been created, made perfect, and finished, is the shoe now worth more than all of its parts? I ask this because just a heel or an insole alone is kind of useless to you, but as a whole, you can put on the shoes and use them. It's worth more now because it is complete.

Take a house being built as an example. Is the land you built your new home on now worth more because now there is a place to live that fulfills a purpose of value versus all of the parts separately? As George S. Clason says, "Wealth grows in magic ways. No man can prophesy the limit of it."[14] Wealth really is created from our creative energies.

Okay, stay with me—I'm not giving you a shoe economics class for my health but only to illustrate a point. Perhaps you are sitting here in a place where you are thinking scarcity, where you think there are limited resources available to us, or you think money is limited, when, in fact we have *limitless* resources available to us—not just because the Federal Reserve seems to print off fiat currency like it's going out of style, but because wealth can be created. Wealth is created every day in various forms. It will multiply for you if you let it, and just start by getting out of the mindset that we live in a place of scarcity. It's not a change in thinking; it will be a transformation of your life when you begin to think this way and uncover what is possible. It is all there in your head, and it flows to the ends of your

---

14 George S. Clason, *The Richest Man in Babylon*, (Lulu.com, 2013), 24.

fingertips and to the tips of your toes! In a great article for *Forbes*, economist Russ Roberts is quoted in a discussion about "pie"—that is, when you're talking about "getting your piece of the pie," you should think again. "[T]he pie is not constant. So your well-being can grow even when your share of the pie falls if the pie is getting sufficiently larger."[15] Wealth is not a zero-sum game. In other words, when I make money, I'm not taking it away from you, and vice versa. Think about this. There is enough money in the world that every-one can be a millionaire without taking away from anyone, because wealth can be created.

As I mentioned already, this chapter is about debt, but I'm not going to ever preach to you about debt because ... I have it, too! In fact, when you have your own business and need equipment, you may always have debt to some degree. In my marriage, my husband has a business where he always has to buy new equipment, and yes, as most businesses go, you do have debt at certain points because you need to raise capital to get the job done. The problem becomes more about how you manage it and whether you can keep it under control—but you already know when it's manageable and when it's out of control.

I want my message to you to be about being kind and forgiving to yourself financially. This is money mercy. Women struggle with forgiveness; we are always the martyrs, and most of us can forgive others easily before we forgive ourselves. Do you find yourself in that camp? If so, this is what you do: say out loud that you forgive your-self. It's so important to speak it and declare your intentions. You will find how easy it is when you stop making it hard for yourself.

The energy that the spoken and written word have is powerful, and when you declare your intentions, they will begin to manifest in your life. So say goodbye to the financial stress of debt and the hold

---

15   Russ Roberts, quoted in Yaron Brook and Don Watkins, "When It Comes to Wealth Creation, There Is No Pie," *Forbes* (June 14, 2011).

it has had over you in your life. Make a plan to pay off your debt, and then in a mob boss voice, say, "Forgeddabouttit." You will find a new sense of freedom and enjoyment in your life, and I'm sure you may even gain a little sparkle in you step.

Here's another way to look at your debt, if you have any. Catherine Ponder suggests in *The Dynamic Laws of Prosperity* that you look at your debt as a blessing—someone entrusted you with funds with the responsibility that you would pay it back.[16]

For your information, when you borrow money, you don't actually borrow from a bank; you borrow from yourself—or, as Preet Banerjee (the host of *Million Dollar Neighbourhood*) says, you are "borrowing from your future self."[17] You take a loan from your future self, and the bank profits. It's so true! It's such a good way to look at debt and one of the reasons you should pay it down as fast as possible. So, yes, don't rob your future self.

In the absence of information, our brain fills in the gaps with other information in our head. You know this: We have a bias—we tend to see what we want to see, and thus create a self-fulfilling prophecy. We always tend to do the opposite of what we are supposed to do. Point in case: I just bought the shoes. Yup, another pair—like I could've invested it, or saved it, or whatever. You all know the phrase—"buy low, sell high," which is the same for shoes as it is stocks. I will talk about this further in the chapter "Running Shoes," regarding investing. Just know the psychological needs will always outweigh any logic.

Here's another reason having a financial coach on your side when working with money is helpful. This goes back to the Solomon Asch Experiment, where participants were given two cards with lines on them and asked which of the lines were the same length. Peer pressure caused the people being experimented on to give in and follow the crowd, when the other participants were told to

16 Catherine Ponder, *The Dynamic Laws of Prosperity*, rev. ed. (Marina del Rey, CA: DeVorss, 1985).

17 Preet Banerjee, "Why 2.5 Billion Heartbeats Might Change the Way You Think About Money," TED Talk, *TEDxUTSC*, February 12, 2013, http://tedtalks.ted.com/video/ Why-2-5-billion-heartbeats-migh.

choose the wrong answer on purpose. The lesson? The crowd isn't always as smart as you and your sixth sense.

Make no mistake, my dear friends, the more you make, the more you spend. Expenses have a magical way of moving in lock-step with an increase in income. So if you are waiting to make more money before you pay down your debt and start putting together a financial plan, think again—start now. Start today.

Advisors (if they are doing their job) are here to save you from your brains, which are hardwired to make bad financial decisions. So if your advisor gives you a rough time about withdrawing your RRSP to pay for a trip or a trip to the mall, then know that he is probably a good advisor to keep around! It's really important to know where we are so that we know where to go.

Don't get stressed out about debt! Remember what you focus on multiplies and manifests in your life: good, bad or ugly! Remember that you can always earn more money if you choose to. Remember the only people that really make money work at the mint!

This is why I do cash flow planning and why I've incorporated it into my business and actually rebuilt my business around it. It's by far the most exciting thing I've seen to date in the financial planning world. Check it out at www.ellementsgroup.com/cashflowplan or go online in your area and find yourself a Certified Cash Flow Specialist!

Why I found cash flow planning so amazingly brilliant is because it's finally something that doesn't require budgeting, and it does incorporate your personality; in other words, it's behavioural psychology!

Budgets are worse than diets. Budgets make you feel fat and "budgie." Ugh! I mean, honestly—how are "we the people" supposed to really follow budgets when our own elected government and corporations don't?

I cringe, too! Because I like Starbucks, purses, *and* shoes (clearly), and I will throw myself off a cliff if I don't get my coffee—let alone let a financial advisor tell me I can't have coffee *and* I have to go on a budget! (Insert profanity of choice.) That would have never happened—*plus* that doesn't get us long-term results. It's because most of our spending is emotional.

Also, it's important to note that this is *not* about financial accomplishments. Accomplishments are like awards you can put on your fireplace mantle that say things like "debt-free" and "Retired with $2,000,000 in assets." Congratulations! Those things are accomplishments. Accomplishments are great. However, they don't lead to a *life you love*. Accomplishments and dreams are not the same thing!

Accomplishments do *ignite;* however, be sure that they are the side effect of *your* dreams and not just a way to brag to the world about how much money you have or to use your wealth as something that glorifies your ego. How soon we forget; you can't leave this world with your cash anyways. And what good does it do you to fill your fireplace full of accomplishment awards?

Dreams are different. Dreams are what *fuel* you. Dreams are the vision you have for your life—the vision to create something worthwhile and to have a positive impact on the world, your community, your family, and your best friend.

Cash flow planning is about *dreams,* not accomplishments. Accomplishments will be the side effect of your cash flow plan. This marks a paradigm shift from the eye-rolling, boring big bank stuff to the exciting things that will change your life and fund your dreams. Cash flow planning is about seeing dreams become reality in less than a few years—definitely sooner than age sixty-five (unless you are sixty-three!). It's about creating balance and accomplishing important stuff now.

Getting your own unique cash flow plan will change the way you think about money, the way you use your money, and the relationship you have with money; a cash flow plan deals with your unique personality, as well as the numbers. It already takes into account the fact that you love your Starbucks coffee and your purses and you don't want to live with a paper bag over your head to make your financial dreams a reality.

I love the study of behavioural finance because it just confirms what we already inherently know. We humans will always take the path of least resistance, and we want instant gratification. Sure, we can overcome this, but at the end of the day, we all come from the same cloth; we want *simple and easy.*

This is why I have found cash flow planning to be awesome, because you:

ↆ   Create financial clarity—figure out why you are "saving" money to begin with.

ↆ   Get more *life* from your money.

ↆ   Reduce financial stress and worry.

ↆ   Start funding your dreams in a real way.

For cash flow planning, you really do need to check out my website. These plans are unique and tailored to you. I would encourage you to find a Certified Cash Flow Specialist in your area. If not, check out my website and learn about this amazing and simple way to get more life from your money, fund your dreams, and create financial clarity.

FUN SHOE FACT: Shoes all over the world were identical until the nineteenth century, when left- and right-footed shoes were first made in Philadelphia. That had to be more comfortable.

SOLE QUOTE: "I would hate for someone to look at my shoes and say, 'Oh my God! They look so comfortable!'" —Christian Louboutin

SOUL QUOTE: "Worry is like paying interest on tomorrow's debt." —Ken Alford

"Being an adult is realizing that $5,000 is a lot of money to owe and very little money to own." —Reddit

Strut

FAB READS:

- *The Richest Man in Babylon* by George S. Clason
- *The Dynamic Laws of Prosperity* by Catherine Ponder
- *The Science of Getting Rich* by Wallace Wattles

SHOUT IT OUT: I am free!

PUTTIN' ON THE SHOES:

- Create a written plan to get out of high-interest consumer debt.
- Try non-conventional ways of earning extra income to get out of debt.
- Check out my cash flow planning resources at www.ellementsgroup.com/cashflowplan.
- Did I mention cash flow planning? Check it out!

SHOEBOX NOTES:

- Debt: nearly six out of ten Canadians retire in debt. Make a plan to not be one of them.
- There is debt (which is annoying, like a blister on your foot), and there is worse debt (likened to an artery bleeding out of control). Find balance, and get control.
- All financial tools have a place, so just know your limits, and keep your eyes on the goal.
- I don't want you to be hard on yourself about debt. I want you to take ownership, make a plan, and move forward.
- Have some money mercy on yourself.
- You don't need to budget, but you do need a cash flow plan.

STRUT TUNES:

- "New Shoes" by Paolo Nutini
- "Walking on Sunshine" by Katrina & The Waves

Lisa Elle

- "No Shoes, No Shirt, No Problem" by Kenny Chesney
- "Who's Gonna Fill Those Shoes" by Buddy Guy

4

Rain Boots

It will rain! It will rain!
Every path has its puddles,
Just make sure you have rain boots
To dance through the muddle.

STYLE DESCRIPTION: An ankle-high overshoe made of plastic or rubber to protect feet from rain and mud.

PROSPERITY DESCRIPTION: Make sure you are protected when it rains, because the sun can't shine every day.

I love a great pair of rain boots, even though it rarely rains hard enough where I live to warrant them. Despite this, I'm still glad I own a pair (or two or three), because I never know when I may unexpectedly need them. It's kind of like insurance (okay—I heard you cringe!).

Insurance is not something anybody *wants* to use, because for most of us, that means the unexpected has happened. However, it's imperative to have insurance for that rare, heavily rainy day.

I'm so excited about this chapter (yes, I may actually be the first person in history of the universe that has been excited to discuss insurance). It's such an important topic, and one that is often misunderstood—for good reason. Most of you would rather be at the dentist right now getting a root canal while being forced to watch a *Keeping Up With the Kardashians* marathon than have to endure one minute of this conversation. The benefit of this being a book is that you can always skip these next few chapters and get to something you're more comfortable with.

That being said, I would encourage you to at least give this chapter a quick read—this insurance knowledge is the foundation to a good financial plan, and I promise I'll try to make it as fun as possible (I may also be the first person to use "insurance" and "fun" in the same sentence).

Imagine this: you buy a brand-new car. It's gorgeous. It's your dream car, and you find you've started liking it more than your husband. You might even go so far as to say you're in love. You take such good care of it; you clean it more often than you do your kids and take it out for scenic country drives. You'd give it the other spot in your bed if you thought it would fit. You know everything about this car, and you've made a significant investment of time, energy, and money that you've put into a beautiful piece of machinery that gives you such a thrill whenever you see it.

But when you bought it at the dealership, you waived the option to purchase the accompanying insurance on it. You tell anyone who questions your decision that you're a good driver and you never get into accidents, and therefore, you find it unnecessary.

Then, two years later, you're out for a drive, decide to park your baby on a country road, and get out to go for a walk. When you return, a huge black bear is sitting on the hood of your car. (Don't laugh—in the mountainous region I live in, this actually isn't that low of a probability.) You watch (from a safe distance, of course) as this magnificent creature sinks its claws into the smooth metal as it attempts to pry open the window you left slightly cracked open for air flow. The window fractures under the pressure, leaving a spider web of cracks. The bear is frustrated and starts to go after the antenna with its teeth, leaving massive dents in the body from the weight of its hind legs.

The beautiful love of your life is now reduced to a worthless heap of metal. "Worthless," only because you refused the insurance, convinced that only sunny days were ahead as there was no rain the forecast.

Bears happen; it's okay. Some of it is so unlikely that it seems funny; some of it's sad, but rainy days filled with illness, disability, and unexpected events happen to all of us, no matter how low we estimate the risks to be. I realize that the most unrealistic aspect of the above scenario (as an aside, please don't seriously value a car over your family) is that most places won't let you buy a car without proof of insurance; however, this example was meant to demonstrate two important points:

1 You never know what's around the corner, be it hungry wildlife or a driver who just isn't paying attention. I was rear-ended at a stop light in a minor incident yesterday. Bears happen; distracted drivers happen—we cannot control external factors. I was not expecting to be rear-ended early Monday morning. The other driver got out, explaining how he had spilled coffee all over himself on the way to work.

2 On a different level of seriousness, it is an entirely common phenomenon to invest more in the protection of stuff than people. It may seem crazy, but if you were to check right now, there's a good chance you are paying more for you home and car insurance than you are for health, disability, or critical illness insurance—which won't probably be changing, but it does show us what we value as a society. We are more worried about our toys and convince ourselves that it's perfectly normal to place higher importance on insuring our $50,000 car than

insuring ourselves (which, by the way, it isn't). You are way more valuable than any car, whether you spent $50,000 or $200,000 on it.

I'm not going to try to sell you on all the insurance you need. I realize every time I sit with clients, price is always going to be a huge consideration, and let's be blunt: insurance isn't cheap. Instead, I'm going to give you my tips when looking for a good policy in order to make sure you get the coverage you need for *you*. We'll cover life insurance in the next chapter.

"Rain boots" are to get you through the puddles so you can continue enjoying life. These are called *living benefits*, because you utilize them only while you are still alive. However, before I cover the areas of living benefits, we need to talk about insurability.

Have you ever been to Costco and said you were going to "grab it later," although you realize later it wasn't there? I've done this about a hundred times.

Enter: The World of Insurability

Insurability, in my terms, is an insurance company's opinion of you, your health, lifestyle, and family history at a certain point in time, typically when applying for insurance.

Here's the thing. When applying for individual health, critical illness, disability, or life insurance, you *need* to get it while you are healthy. It's this crazy thing where insurance companies don't want to take on your smoking, drinking, diabetic, deep-fried-Oreo-eating habits (all the things that make for a great, *great* Stampede week in Calgary!). I think this has something to do with their business model emphasizing profits.

I had a client call me yesterday. He told me he had just had a stroke and in the next breath mentioned how glad he was to have purchased his life insurance last year (and I have heard hundreds of stories like this). Any of my clients who have had living benefits claims say the same thing: they wished they had more insurance.

So what do you do? Get your insurance while you are young and healthy—and apply preferably before Stampede or Christmas vacation.

If you are uninsurable, policies are still available, but premiums are higher. Find an insurance broker/agent/advisor who specializes in traditional underwriting (the kind where you have to take medical tests and have a nurse come over—preferable if you are in good health), or non-traditional underwriting (policies that ask you only healthy questions and base underwriting decisions instantly on your answers). The non-traditional insurance market offers insurance products for *everyone* ... although again, this means higher premiums and smaller payouts. However, most people don't even know that's an option, *and* most insurance brokers don't, either.

Lucky for you, I specialize in both. I can answer any of your "boring" insurance questions. I'm serious—contact me. (I slept with an insurance textbook under my pillow for fifteen years.)

You never know what tomorrow holds for you and your family. I still laugh when people say, "Well, my parents lived to a hundred, kicking and healthy." If that's the story that keeps you warm at night, then I wish you sweet dreams. Reality is this:

49: This is the *average* age of all critical illness claims in Canada (yes, "average," meaning half younger and half older).

56: That is the *average* age of widowhood in Canada (meaning your man should not be your retirement plan).

So do yourself a solid favour and get a few million dollars of life insurance on the good ol' hubby, because that story will keep you warm at night. When God takes hubby, he will leave behind a Golden Gucci Purse to cuddle with or a nice pair of Choos.

I poke fun, but bear with me, and forgive my strange brand of humour; I sell life insurance for a living. What I mean to say is this: you may not die tomorrow, but your insurability and the options to get a great policy might die tomorrow, so get the proper coverage today while you are healthy.

There are four main types of living benefits: healthcare insurance, critical illness insurance, disability insurance, and travel insurance. I'll review these areas and provide you with key questions to ask your insurance companies, agents, or advisors to ensure you have the most cost-effective policy with the proper type of coverage for you.

I can't overemphasize the importance of making sure you are comfortable with the monthly payments, because the only good insurance policy or financial plan is the one that you keep. If you are missing payments or have to cancel the plan, it is of no value to you. It's better to choose a middle-of-the-road policy you can maintain versus being talked into a shiny, fancy plan with all the bells and whistles that is unfeasible to keep. Think of it as choosing a more sensible, comfortable pair of shoes to go the distance at Saturday night's party, rather than the knockout diamond-studded platform heels you can last maybe two hours in before you finally toss them to the side, thus choosing to go barefoot instead.

Let's first review the difference between term and permanent policies, because all types and forms of insurance can fall into one of these camps.

Term insurance refers to a policy that is valid for a set period, be it one year or a hundred years. When we are discussing health insurance or travel insurance, we need to note these policies are all one-year terms, just like car or home insurance. The premiums or price you pay will adjust slightly every year.

Actuaries—the really smart, number-crunching people—run scenarios based on past claims experience to make sure the insurance companies are operating in the black. And here you thought for a minute that insurance companies provided their services out of the goodness of their hearts! That's sweet. Don't worry: the actuaries do a very good job at making sure the insurance companies' bank accounts are taken care of. We could all learn a thing or two from risk management.

Term is the most common type of life and critical illness insurance sold in Canada, which are typically ten-year or twenty-year terms, although they can be any pre-set time frame. This means your policy rate—the price you pay every month—stays the same for the duration of that term. Once that term is complete, you typically have four options:

1 Cancel the policy. These policies do not typically have cash value associated with them.

2 Renew the policy at the renewal rates stated in your original policy. This usually means a significant increase, and you would usually take this route only if you are ill and unable to qualify for new insurance otherwise.

3 Rewrite a new policy. However, this requires new evidence of insurability—or, in real-girl talk, you need to be healthy to qualify and redo your medicals. Typically, this rate is more than what you were previously paying per month but less expensive than if you kept your current policy and faced the renewal rates.

4 Convert your policy to permanent insurance. All term insurance policies do eventually expire—most at age seventy-five or eighty, as an example—but typically, up to age sixty-five, you can convert to permanent insurance. This insurance will last to age one hundred.

In the permanent life insurance camp, there are three main types of permanent insurance: term to age a hundred, whole life, and a universal life. There are also permanent critical illness policies to age one hundred or to age seventy-five, and a plethora of riders (add-on benefits to your policy, such as a waiver of premium in the event of disability, for example) or add-ons to those policies as well.

With all policies, it is important to note no one is better than another. Typically, for my clients with younger families, I recommend term insurance, and for older clients, I recommend a smaller permanent policy. It's worth mentioning again the best policy is one that you keep and eventually pays out you or your beneficiaries.

When it comes to disability insurance, typically it is term up to age sixty-five or seventy, which is developed to assist you until you retire and is meant to provide coverage while you are working. If you want disability insurance, you need to be earning income to get a policy. It is not designed for the unemployed. On that note, critical illness insurance does not have an income requirement, so many people—such as stay- or work-at-home moms and children—are able to qualify for it as well.

Extended Healthcare Insurance

We are fortunate to have access to fantastic healthcare, minus all the aches and complaints portrayed in the media and all the political rigmarole around the subject. Private or public, take a moment to appreciate that and hug a nurse or doctor next time you see one, and thank her for what she does, because many countries long for the services of nurses or doctors, and we can utilize when necessary.

Here's an amusing anecdote for you: I even thanked my gynaecologist the other day, because I love expressing gratitude while my legs are in the stirrup position. You just can't put a price tag on that awkward moment and nervous laugh. Despite the uncomfortable nature of the situation, I was grateful because I don't have to pay her directly out of pocket. In my case, my province pays for the clamp-and-swab treatment, as well as many other wonderful services.

However, the province does not cover everything: prescriptions, dental work, and eye exams are just a few of my own responsibilities. In fact, the list of what public health does *not* cover gets longer every year.

Many of us (or a spouse or partner) work for an employer who may cover all or part of our extended healthcare plan. If you are self-employed, the responsibility of an extended healthcare plan falls on you, but the good news is you can deduct the premiums from your taxable income.

There aren't many companies that offer this type of plan, but there are a few for every province. If you have your own corporation, you have the option of a Private Health Services Plan (PHSP). A PHSP takes any medical expenses incurred by you or your employees and turns it into a tax deduction for the corporation. At the end of the day, the corporation is paying for the expense regardless, but this is just an avenue to turn the expense into a deduction. So if you are going to get laser eye surgery anyway, you may as well be able to deduct it.

I often hear the rebuttal from those who figure that for what they pay in premiums, they may as well forego a plan and just pay for the dentist or the prescription when they need it. It's true for the expected services such as a dentist appointment, massage, chiropractic treatments, and so forth, you will typically break even for the services you use. However, this is not the kind of insurance meant for those services you can anticipate but rather for the unexpected occurrence, so you will have the coverage you need. It's for the things such as emergency dental work, ambulance rides, or being diagnosed with an illness that requires medication for life. That is when you'll fully appreciate the pay-offs.

Here's another point to note about this type of coverage: you can get extended healthcare only if you are healthy. If you are not, some basic plans are available, but for the most part, you need to already have a plan in place should your health change. For example, if you have no plan in place and are given a diabetes diagnosis that will require medication, an insurance company may issue you a policy with a diabetes medication exclusion, offer you a substandard plan, or just decline you altogether. It is so important to note that if you have a plan through your employer and you leave your job, you are able to switch your plan over to your own personal plan within thirty or sixty days of departure. It may or may not be with another carrier, and you will be paying the premiums for it, but it may be your only option. If you already require an ample supply of pills, you will have no other choice. Again, insurance companies tend to favour healthy people.

It is essential to make sure you have your foundation covered with a solid, basic extended healthcare plan—this is definitely a situation where the rhinestones should not be your primary focus. PHSPs (Private Health Service Plans) are great for being able to deduct your expenses if you have a business, but you still need to have a great insurance plan in place. I encourage both options for those who are self-employed. If you have a corporation, you need to have a PHSP.

Like the process of finding a pair of shoes that fits you just right, you also need to shop around for insurance. Depending on what services you use and don't use, insurance advisors, like myself, can tailor plans to meet your specific needs.

Critical Illness

In Canada, only 3 percent of Canadians have a critical illness policy. I'm willing to bet most of you don't actually know what critical illness insurance is—and that's okay! Even the people who *do* know often don't fully understand the power of what it can do for you and your family.

Critical insurance is a lump sum, tax-free payout you receive when diagnosed with a critical illness, such as a heart attack, cancer, or stroke, and typically up to twenty-five to thirty illnesses. There is typically a waiting period of thirty days up to three months for some illnesses. The largest claim by far is cancer, with approximately 80 percent of all claims, and the average age for all claims is forty-two years old. Forty-two! Average! This is not a type of insurance you want to wait to get. Like all insurance, the younger you are, the cheaper it is.

The critical illness payout provides income or money for private healthcare, the ability to travel the world for the best doctors and treatments and avoid queue, pay off your house or some debt, create memories on a family trip, cover wigs or medical home renovations, supplement work income or protecting your nest egg or retirement accounts while you recover, or even to fulfill a lifelong dream. The possibilities are endless. You wouldn't want to be tied to your desk if you were to be diagnosed with a critical illness, and the same goes if it happened to a loved one.

And here's the thing: critical illnesses are no longer a death sentence. Thanks to advancements in the medical industry, many people live several years after a heart attack or a cancer diagnosis and subsequent remission. Excitingly, we are starting to see that progress.

The term versions of these policies are relatively inexpensive in comparison to disability insurance, and you can get small face amounts, such as $10,000 or $25,000. In my experience, policies of $100,000 to $250,000 policies are most common amongst the average Canadian. You also do not usually have to prove income for most policies; however, they will always ask anyway (you do *not* have to disclose how much you spend annually on your shoe collection—I asked).

There are even policies that don't require evidence of insurability, as well as many new policy types in Canada. You need to ask a good insurance advisor who knows the realm of both traditional and non-traditional underwriting, or someone who knows the guaranteed issue market of the insurance world. Find someone who is able to navigate that territory and explore all of your options, because there technically is a critical illness policy out there for everyone—even if you've had a heart attack or cancer in the past.

Disability Insurance

You are six times more likely to be disabled than to die. How's that for a cheery opener to this subject? For the most part, a good disability policy will be the most expensive of all your policies. Disability insurance will provide you with a monthly income while you are out of commission. This income is usually tax-free, so insurance companies typically provide you with 60 to 70 percent of your taxable income, which means you will receive slightly less than you would while working. In other words, disability insurance is not a get-rich-quick (or at all) scheme; however, you should be able to maintain your quality of life.

If you can afford only either critical illness insurance or disability insurance, choose the latter. But if both are viable options, remember that disability insurance is usually not enough coverage to cover potential necessities like home modification, additional surgeries, private healthcare, or medications that aren't covered by your health plan.

One very popular route explored by many attempting to treat illnesses is non-traditional medicines and healthy eating. This will not be covered by any insurance company, and a diet and lifestyle using non-traditional methods can be very expensive. This is where the lump sum payout of critical illness insurance becomes very important.

Travel Insurance

Travel insurance may already be part of your extended health-care group plan through work. Whether it is or isn't, do not even consider leaving your country—maybe even your province—without it. It is very inexpensive if you are under sixty-five; however, once you hit the magic age, it is no longer nearly as reasonable, hence why it is the number-one reason snowbirds stop heading south for the winter.

You do not want to be caught in the United States or any other country without emergency medical insurance. I can tell you horror stories, and everyone knows of at least one themselves.

I was recently at my annual work conference in San Francisco (actually, I'm writing this from my beautiful hotel room). It was amazing—five-star all the way. I wined and dined at all the classiest iconic places in town. My thirty-five-year-old body is quickly realizing it's not eighteen anymore, and four days of rich foods and wine start to kick in—just like my credit card statement will kick in after this whole US/CND exchange-rate fiasco—as I typically don't eat or drink like that at home (I'm a pretty healthy girl for the most part!).

I get back to my hotel room at midnight, and I can't sleep. I think I have indigestion or food poisoning. Perhaps it was the shrimp. No, maybe the oysters. No, maybe the steak. Geez. The cheese platter? That last gin and tonic. (Honestly, we start at 5:00 p.m. and go till midnight—a lot happens in seven hours of eating and drinking for several days straight.) Then it hits me. It *must* have been the pork belly on that cute crouton with the yummy aioli sauce shaped like a heart....

As I'm contemplating what foods I ate, I realize my pain is increasing, and it's like nothing I've felt before. Okay, lies. It felt like the end stages of child labour—been there and got the T-shirt!

So with no sleep, at 5:00 a.m. and in excruciating pain, I call my Canadian travel insurance company's phone number and ask where I should go to seek medical attention. The representative gives me the name and address and off I stumble down through the lobby. I grab a taxi to the hospital emergency.

They were waiting for me at the California Pacific Medical Centre. They knew I was coming. It was quite nice, sort of like checking into a hotel (I have to say, minus my pain, the whole experience was rather quite enjoyable).

Eight hours later, after a page-long list of pain medications I can't pronounce, a CT scan, an ultrasound, blood work, and all diagnostics completed, I was diagnosed with a gall bladder attack, which subsided hours later. Honestly, I was terrified that it was a heart attack, because the symptoms for both are similar—thankfully, it wasn't. I was told to stay off fatty foods, and on my way back to the hotel I was feeling a million times better.

And the happy part of the story is that they billed my emergency medical travel insurance directly, and the only time I had to open my wallet was for my prescription medication; however, they will be reimbursing me for that, too. I could go on about private healthcare and what a wonderful experience it was with no queue. The customer service was amazing. Ohhh—I had a hot doctor, too (Hi, Dr. Dan), so that helped. I felt like I was in my own episode of *Grey's Anatomy*. And I digress....

I'm so happy that, overall, the tests showed that I'm in great health (a huge blessing). I'm feeling great and reminding everyone who travels out of province and out of country to purchase travel insurance. As I said above, it's relatively inexpensive if you are under sixty-five, but all it takes is one tiny incident and you could be paying for it big time, cashing in investments you have worked hard to save up, re-mortgaging your home, or worse.

Funny enough, I'm staying at the hotel where Tony Bennett sang his famous song "I Left My Heart in San Francisco." I'm just glad I had travel insurance to cover this, or I'd be singing "I left my money in San Francisco."

And do you know what the final bill of my eight-hours-in-San-Fran-ER-somebody-kill-me-now-I-feel-like-I'm-having-a-baby gall-bladder attack came to? $16,662.97 CND!

Just make sure you know exactly what you have covered, and for how many days, and for how much. Coverage up to $1 million to $5 million is standard, and it's so simple to obtain; you can buy it online. Seriously. I even sell it on my website (if you are in

Canada). It's easy to do, and you can purchase it up to the day you leave the country. I won't tell you how many times I've had clients call me as they are on their way to the airport. Funnily enough, it's the same people that call me on March 1 for their annual RRSP contribution!

If you are pregnant, you need to have a doctor's note to travel if you are close to your due date. Travelling against doctor's order could render your policy void, so can pre-existing conditions if you get hospitalized while away. Best to talk with a licensed insurance advisor about your conditions before you go. Also, try not to buy from the "corner store," and if you do have questions, don't buy travel insurance online like I mentioned above—call me instead. It's better to have all your health questions answered before you buy blinded.

Get a good insurance advisor who is able to represent the market to find you policies that will best suit your needs. Your advisor knows the underwriting requirements and, based on your job, income, and health, will be able to steer you in the right direction.

FUN SHOE FACT: Dorothy's ruby red slippers from *The Wizard of Oz* are insured for $1 million, and Judy Garland wore four different pairs in the film.

SOLE QUOTE: "I hate spending money on shoes ... but the economy needs me!" —Unknown

SOUL QUOTE: "If you fail to plan, you are planning to fail." —Benjamin Franklin

"Do something today that your future self will thank you for." —Unknown

Lisa Elle

FAB READS:
On insurance? Ha! I'm not going to bore you, dear friend. However, if you have insomnia, your local insurance council's textbook is always a good nighttime read. It's better to email me any questions via my website at www.ellements-group.com. I can help you sort through this fascinating topic, or at least point you in the right direction.

SHOUT IT OUT: I am *strong*.

PUTTIN' ON THE SHOES:

- Meet with your life and living benefits insurance advisor (or your amazing financial coach or financial planner) for a full review at least every few years, or when a major life event occurs, such as a baby, wedding, divorce, or death—or every time you buy new shoes.

- To sell living benefits, your advisor must have an Accident and Sickness License. It is also helpful if they also have a Life Insurance License.

- Make sure your life and living benefits insurance advisor represents a variety of insurance companies and offers life, critical illness, disability, and health insurances (my advice will be the same for the next chapter, too!).

- A person in Canada who has any planning designation such as a CFP (Certified Financial Planner) or CHS (Certified Health Specialist) or CLU (Chartered Life Underwriter) is a good choice for a financial coach in this arena.

SHOEBOX NOTES:

- Make sure you know what coverage you have!

- No question is a stupid question—remember the insurance lingo was developed just to make insurance licensing exams hard to pass.

- Make sure to consult an insurance advisor regarding when you are leaving your group benefits behind, because insurability and health are very important.

- Underwriting is a jungle—that's the value of a good insurance advisor. Plus, in most cases, you can't purchase a policy in Canada without an advisor/agent—although that is changing, and you can buy online with no advice, which is more work for you.

Strut

➤ Good policies are underwritten upfront, with minimal underwriting at time of claim.

➤ Just remember, you are here to live, and when finding yourself in a discouraging health or debilitative situation, keep in mind how much easier that situation could be if you didn't have to worry about money coming in each month to pay your expenses.

➤ It's about planning for the expected and being prepared for the unexpected.

STRUT TUNES:

➤ "Those Shoes" by Eagles

➤ "Shoes" by Shania Twain

➤ "Pretty Woman" by Roy Orbison

➤ "In These Shoes" by Helena Jessie

5

Winter Boots

*What good is the warmth of summer without the cold
of winter to give it sweetness?*
—John Steinbeck

STYLE DESCRIPTION: A strong heavy shoe reaching the ankle or above, keeping feet warm and dry in snow.

PROSPERITY DESCRIPTION: Planning ahead for the winters of your life to ease the cold.

I **choose winter** boots to represent the hard winters we walk through in life in regards to the loss of a loved one. The inevitable is just that, and after selling life insurance for over fifteen years, you have to have some fun with it; otherwise, life insurance salespeople would have a higher suicide rate than dentists. We will all be there one day. We all came into this world, and we all will depart at some point— this is why I call it "departure insurance." It is always part of a good financial plan. When you depart, what are you leaving behind? And who do you want to be the beneficiary of all your hard work?

Insurance companies thought "life" insurance sounded better than "death" insurance—for marketing purposes, of course. Nobody wants to think about that, anyways; in order to survive, we as humans basically pretend death doesn't exist most of the time, so imagine selling it! No kid says, "I want to sell life insurance when I grow up." At kindergarten graduation over the last few years, I had one daughter who said she wanted to be a doctor and one who wanted to be Aurora (yes, the princess—it was a proud mommy moment). No kid got up to the microphone and said they wanted to be a financial planner or sell life insurance. I started selling life insurance by default because it was easier to ease into the financial planning business with a life insurance licence; so with *zero* desire to sell life insurance, over fifteen years later, I now know the benefits of life insurance and have seen firsthand what the money does for the families left behind. I have personally delivered eight cheques, and although each time is hard, you can see the relief in the families' eyes when they know they don't have to be financially burdened while bearing the loss of a loved one.

Life insurance is more a talk about options versus getting rich from a loved one. So many of us were raised to believe that money is the root of all evil. If you are part of that *boot* camp, then I hope you take one thing from this book. I want you to full-heartedly know money is not bad; it is good. It is a tool and means of exchange. We could still be trading in sheep, or maybe shoes—how much fun would that be? But above all, money creates options for your life. It makes you more of who you are. I don't believe it changes you; it amplifies you.

When faced with the loss of a loved one, it's nice to have options. You will want to throw that person one hell of a sending-off party and not be worried about the gas bill and mortgage payment due the next week or depleting your assets at an inopportune time.

With young families, I usually recommend a larger term insurance policy, a hybrid policy, or both term and permanent. They are affordable and provide the coverage needed at a great cost. For older clients, I usually recommend only permanent policies. They tend to be more costly. But at the end of the day, you should have the type of insurance that fits your situation. This is where a good independent insurance advisor will come in handy. (And truth be told, the insurance that usually gets sold is the policy the clients can afford, so affordability usually trumps what insurance the client actually needs most of the time.)

The question every advisor always gets asked is this: How much life insurance do I need? And there are formulas, spreadsheets, calculators, and opinions up the wazoo. But I keep it simple. When sitting with a couple, which is usually the case with life insurance, I say to the wife, "Here's a blank cheque. Your husband can't talk at this point because we are pretending he's not here. How much do you think you will need to run this household, pay off debts, live the lifestyle you are accustomed to (or change your lifestyle to suit your new situation), and get your kids outta the house? Keep in mind that you get only one cheque, and it has to last you for a very long time."

So now I ask you the same. A million dollars does not buy much in the Alberta economy. Maybe it does in yours, but insurance companies always see policies go through for $1 million or $2 million, so don't feel it's an unreasonable amount to insure an income-producing contributing member of your family. Men are getting this concept, too! They realize a homemaker will cost them about $20,000 to $30,000 per year to get the basics done, like maintaining a clean house, preparing some meals, and getting the laundry done. Childcare is a huge expense for young families as well.

So that's it! That's the magic formula. Although, many tools are absolutely helpful to get you thinking about possible future expenses, but at the end of the day, it also boils down to one thing: can you afford the monthly premiums? You might want a $3 million policy, but it may cost you $500 a month, and maybe that's out of your price range; plus, you do need to provide reasons why you require this insurance to insurance companies, and they usually don't insure for $3 million when one is a NINJA, which stands for no income, no job or assets (you can thank the great recession of 2008 for that acronym!).

I know we already covered insurability; however, you need to apply for insurance even when you are healthy. If you are coming to your insurance advisor close to your departure, you probably will not be getting departure insurance. But you come to us when you are healthy or even semi-healthy, and we can work with that. If you have a major health condition, then we can get you insurance; it will just be smaller amounts, typically $100,000 or less.

Never cancel a policy unless the new one is in force. Again, a good policy is underwritten upfront, and yes, that typically takes one to two months (nowadays—some faster), and I've had many policies that can take up to four to six months to underwrite. The second an insurance company has to request information from your family doctor or a hospital, it can take forever. So keep that in mind, too, and don't get ill in the meantime. Insurance is serious business (and it's boring!), but once you have a policy, you are usually good. If something does happen to you and you become uninsurable—and yes, many people are for various reasons—then you can convert your policy or just keep it as is for a while. Remember, they are not just underwriting your health but your family history and your life-style as well.

There are many things to consider while getting life insurance, so it's always best to go with an independent advisor who can best direct you to the best policy that you will get approved for and for the best rates. It's kind of like a fantastic mortgage broker who will shop for the best mortgage rate for you but also a lender who will approve you with your slightly scary credit score or find you a B-rated lender to get the job done. Sometimes a mortgage is better than none, and that's definitely the case with life insurance; it's better to have an approved policy than a declined one and having to wait two years before you can apply again. And yes, if you get declined for a policy in Canada, you pretty much have to wait two years to apply again, unless there are extenuating circumstances around your case. This is why a broker who knows the ins-and-outs is good to have.

And keep this fact in mind: your insurance broker doesn't get paid until you get your insurance policy approved and in force, so it's definitely in their best interest to get you approved. Don't hide health facts from them. If they know all the pertinent information about your health, they can shop and fight as best as they can to get you a policy that best suits you.

Man, I feel like I'm writing a textbook sometimes. If you made it this far, please fix yourself a strong drink. But before you do, one last thought.

Life insurance provides for families in hard times, and this is probably why most people buy it. However, it also provides legacies for communities and charities. Some people buy life insurance policies just to fund their lifelong visions and fund amazing endeavours. So don't limit your thinking when it comes to life insurance. Maybe you couldn't save a million dollars, but you had a policy that could contribute those funds to your lifelong purpose or dream and leave your mark on the world that way, and that's important!

FUN SHOE FACT: Shoe dreams deal with walking certain paths in our lives. If you are wearing tight shoes, the road you are travelling is hard, and much sorrow is involved. Comfortable shoes indicate you are in a good place in your life and that success is around the corner. [Dreaming of] buying shoes indicates you still have quite a distance to travel until you reach your goals. Dirty, worn-down shoes encourage you to examine your spiritual walk or ask you to take a walk of faith.

SOLE QUOTE: "To take the road less travelled, I'll need new boots." —Rue Lala

SOUL QUOTE: "Life is too short to wear boring shoes." —Lisa Elle

FAB READS:
No reading tonight! Your assignment is to engage your family in a great conversation. Sitting with your family and talking about life insurance and funeral planning doesn't sound like Friday Night Family Fun, but a conversation and creating a safe place to talk about your family's goals and dreams naturally brings about estate planning. Whether you're an adult family or young family, next time you're around the dinner table, try to spark a dialogue about the legacies or ways in which you want to leave the world a better place to your children, or ways in which you want to leave it better than you found it. This will get the family talking, create some excitement about living life in the present, and as a by-product, you will find out what's important to your family and can thus make better decisions about what you want to leave behind, who you want to leave it to, and how to do that. It all starts with conversation and an open mind.

Did you know that LIMRA (Life Insurance Marketing and Research Association) says life insurance ownership in Canada is at the lowest level it's been in the last thirty years? This is probably due to cost and insurability. Forty-five percent of Canadians surveyed said that they need more insurance.

SHOUT IT OUT: I live the life I was called to live.

PUTTIN' ON THE SHOES:

- Meet with your insurance advisor to complete a full review of your life insurance.
- Make sure to ask a lot of questions to fully understand your specific policy. Don't worry: you'll forget in a year or two anyways, so take notes. These policies are usually around for a long time.
- Do a simple calculation as to what funds you will need if your partner is not around, or if you are alone raising a family for a number of years. This is very subjective with no right or wrong answer!
- **Get your copy *of The Ultimate Guide to Life Insurance – 10 Must Know Tips for Canadian*s – my FREE quick and easy e-book by going to www.ellementsgroup.com/gettheguide.**

SHOEBOX NOTES:

ꞈ   Get a great insurance broker or advisor to steer you toward the policy that's right for you.

ꞈ   Get life insurance while you are young and healthy (and insurable)!

ꞈ   Start having the hard conversations now versus later, when it's awkward.

STRUT TUNES:

ꞈ   "Dancing Shoes" by The Ginn Sisters

ꞈ   "Shoes" by Patsy Cline

ꞈ   "Let's Face the Music and Dance" by Diana Krall

ꞈ   "Sunday Morning" by Maroon 5

6

Cowboy Boots

*Ahh ... but then there was love, and any girl
knows ... The greatest of these is love ...*

STYLE DESCRIPTION: A style of boot that has a pointed toe, chunky slanted heel, and extends mid-calf; usually leather with decorative stitching or tooling, traditionally worn by cowboys.

PROSPERITY DESCRIPTION: The boots that are under your bed rule your heart, and in many cases, also your wallet.

I had so much resistance writing this chapter. It's by far the toughest subject to write on, give advice on, or even to make beneficial suggestions for. Every relationship has so many different dynamics and without fabulous communication in place, relationships can get really fiery fast when it comes to money—sometimes to the point of non-recovery (money is still one of the biggest reasons for divorce), or to a place where one person in the relationship gives up and just rolls with the punches in order to keep the peace. (Your heart just screamed "Oh, that's so me!" if you are the peacekeeper!)

I have one intention for this chapter: to get the financial conversation started and flowing in your relationship. I know in most relationships today, it's not flowing as easily as it could be. From many years of sitting across the table from couples of all ages, I find that typically, in every relationship, there is one wrangler—you know, the one who takes the reins financially—and then there's typically one person who really doesn't need to pay too much attention, because the other partner is taking care of all that money stuff. It's rare to see both with full-out knowledge of what is going on in their financial situation. As a caveat to that, I do see this dynamic more in the second (or third, etc.) marriages, where both partners seem to be more keenly aware of their financial situation and they are nearing retirement age.

I call the financially interested ones in a relationship the "money honey," mostly because anyone reckless enough to take the financial reins and manage the day-to-day finances in the relationship should be lovingly called "honey." Hence why the hands-off-finances person I refer to as the opposite, "honey money," because they typically ask, "Honey, where's the money?"

We create these defined roles in our relationships naturally so that we can work together, which is smart, but having defined roles isn't really where the battle of the money relationship occurs.

You know in shows when they have the devil on one shoulder and the angel on the other, both whispering different advice into a person's ear when they are stuck and trying to make a decision that they really don't want to make? I think this is really what goes on in our internal dialogue in regards to financial decisions. Well, it does for me, anyways. Maybe not as dramatic as on TV, but every time you are faced with a financial decision, feelings take over and perhaps a little justification. (Okay, it's true—I could justify my way out of my 197th pair of shoes!) We know how to accomplish our financial goals. Anyone can do math and tell you to spend less than you make. If it were that easy, everyone would be a walking multi-millionaire, but money is emotional. It's our feelings towards money that makes our decisions, and when we are in relationships and one person wants to buy a fancy watch while the other person wants to buy new shoes (this has really never happened to me before!), we have to make hard decisions to allocate resources in the most effective way to benefit the relationship as a whole. This dynamic will be part of every aspect of your life as a couple—what house to buy, cars you can afford, insurance policies, etc. This is a never-ending topic that continues on in life, even when you are deciding which nursing home to pay for.

Bottom line: as long as you are in a relationship, money will be a main subject that you will have to face on a daily basis with your partner (the topic of mothers-in-law can be limited to major holidays.)

The subject of money is (ideally) where acts of sacrifice and feelings of love have to take over. However, we have greedy, selfish little minds, and that's just our default setting as humans (I'm by no mean saying that's the way it should stay!), and being able to function in a healthy financial relationship—regardless of financial status—requires trust, sacrifice, patience, communication, and love. I think without those ingredients, you will probably struggle in financial and other areas of your relationship.

Here's a short fairy tale for you. Once upon a time, we have Clive and Suzy, your parents, who fall in love, get married, and nine months later, there you are. (See, I said it was short.)

You grow up in this home watching your parents interact around money, and the way they handle it either becomes your "financial anchor" around all things financial *or* it becomes your mission to do everything the opposite of what your parents taught you because you do not want to end up like them; this, too, could become your "financial anchor."

Our "financial anchors" are what we base all our decisions on. We ask ourselves: will this purchase help us to obtain our financial goals? Often you progress into a partnership or relationship where you both naturally have your own anchors, and sometimes the anchors crash into each other. I think that over many years in a relationship, you *do* create new "financial anchors" as a couple; however, it takes several years to accomplish that.

And here's the *real* deal with relationships and money: you have to be aware and ever-so-cognisant and understanding of your partner's past "financial anchors" around money and the relationship he has with money. You need to create the space for mutual respect and mutual admiration in your relationship.

One specific couple I know came from two different financial and socioeconomic upbringings. The woman told me one day that it was very hard because she was a great saver and he was a spender (I'm sure this rings true with most couples!). When we delved further into their relationship around money, we began to realize it was because he was raised poor and never had heat or sometimes food as a child, so now that they were "making good money," he wanted to spend it all because he felt he deserved it and that was his reason for working so hard. Also, saving money was something he had never witnessed firsthand. Conversely, she was raised in an upper-class family and had no fear around having her basic needs met and her parents saved most of their money. Thus, she was able to save easily, and she didn't feel the need to spend every last cent because she knew she had money in the bank to buy food for the next few years if she wasn't working.

These are two very different upbringings, so it wasn't surprising that how they valued money was so opposite and caused tension in their relationship at times. This is where having an open mind, patience, and understanding comes into play.

Food for thought: do you think that your financial disagreements in your relationship stem from different modes of "financial anchoring"? Is there a way to put yourself in your partner's shoes and try to see things from his view?

Relationships often have two directions they can go. They can be flourishing, or they can be hiding in a shoebox under your bed, stuffed with receipts that the other person doesn't know about. (Oh, come on—like you've never hid a receipt from your husband or paid cash for half of your shoe purchase and the other half on the credit card so the shoes really didn't look that expensive on the receipt?)

It's the same with money and relationships—there are only two routes. You can keep everything totally separate, or you can work as a team. Neither is right, and neither is wrong. The only thing it *has* to be is mutually agreed upon in order for it to work and not interfere with your relationship and love for one another (if you are so lucky as to have that in your life!).

When I asked my dad about what advice he would give regarding relationships and money, my mom immediately chirped in and said, "Dad would say write a contract!" Yes, Dad would say that. In an ideal right-brain world, Type A people, the Myers-Briggs Green people, would all concur—let's write out a contract and state our roles in relationships to money. Like, you do the shopping, you handle the banking and the filing of statements and manage all small financial decisions, and I'll pay the bills, plan out our investments, and handle the larger financial decisions. Wow, that sounds great and perfect for a business relationship. So if you both can stomach it, write a contract. However, I'm guessing that probably *won't* fly with most couples.

But, when my dad gave his "real" advice to me, he said both couples should talk about their strengths and weaknesses around money. *Wow! What a fantastic idea*, I thought. *Who does that? I don't think my husband and I ever had a talk about that.* Actually, I know we have *never* talked about that, mostly, because I feel my weaknesses outweigh my strengths by a long shot (or a shoe closet!).

Money is an ever-changing thing. It is always in motion to some extent, and the dynamics and outside influences around it are always changing. Goals change, as do people's skill and knowledge around handling money, such as learning how money works, what it does, and what your relationship to it is. Self-reflection mixed with open communication will benefit you greatly in the area around money.

After meeting so many couples over the years, I know very typically, men tend to handle most of the big financial matters in relationships and women tend to manage the smaller, day-to-day stuff. Also, I've noticed more and more women are beginning to get on board and take notice. This is so important, and the main message of this chapter—and really, of my book—is to begin to take notice, and not be left in the dark when you find yourself "lone on the range." Cowboys may saunter into your life, walk out of your life, get shot, or you may kick them outta your saloon (with really cute, sexy, super pointy-tipped cowboy boots). But at some point, be it soon or when you are eighty, for women, there is a 97 percent chance that, at some point in your life, you will be on your own for at least a little while. How do you prepare for that? Or if you are there already, how do you work with that? And if you have the perfect cowboy, how do you make sure not to lose your financial brain in his boots?

Love and money: this can be a never-ending chapter because it plays with our heartstrings and also because of the stupid, *stupid* things we do with our money when it comes to the "L" word. Logic will never win out in this argument—which is another point I want to make with money in general. We as people will usually choose the route of instant gratification. That's okay. Be okay with that. Just keep planting seeds away in the background of your life, and you will get the harvest you want out of life.

Let me tell you of some of the stupid things me and my girl-friends have done with money for a guy:

- Paid for a guy's dinner and Ikea furniture, and then he disappeared.

- Bought a guy tickets to his favourite sports team, and he took a guy instead of you.

- Lent a guy money to go on a trip, which he then used to buy tickets for him and his other girlfriend.

- Invested $25,000 in a romantic interest's start-up business, from which he took the money, travelled to Europe, met a girl, and dropped off the face of the planet.

- Called long distance from Germany, with a Canadian calling card routed through Canada to the United States in 1998. The result was a $1,412 phone bill that Mom and Dad had to pay … all because she missed her boyfriend. Whoopsies!

Blessings in disguise, truly—I mean, who would want to end up with one of these lovelies? Oh, the lessons learned in love! (Okay, the phone bill was my fault – what can I say? I was a love-sick seventeen-year-old!)

Balancing the books is hard. Somehow, even the biggest and brightest governments can't seem to get it right, and then they expect the people to get it. Not to mention they expect a man and a woman—who couldn't be more opposite to begin with—to actually agree on this stuff. So maybe it's time to re-soul your cowboy boots and step into the horseshit. Sit down with your partner and start talking about the big things in your financial world. It's going to be messy, and if you are lucky, it will end in great make-up sex. It's a funny thing; couples usually choose to begin fighting right when sitting down with their financial planner. We have a knack for bringing out the big fights around money. I've definitely had my share of awkward moments!

Wouldn't it be great to have couples' financial meditative yoga or couples' financial massages, where you go in and talk about money in a relaxed manner? That probably doesn't exist in real life, so when you do decide to start talking about money, take four deep breaths and then begin calmly.

One big tip for couples is this: if you do pool your money, then you should each allocate some monthly "fun money" so you do not have to tell your partner where the money went—a.k.a no strings attached. You can spend yours on shoes; he can spend his on beer and golf. This is where the cash flow plans I offer are brilliant and uniquely personalized and can help define your fun money while still making sure you are on target to reach your financial goals.

Because my goal for this chapter is to get the conversation flowing, I have an amazing set of questions you can sit down and go through as a couple, on a date, or in a public place (for safety's sake—just in case you have one excitable person in your relationship!).

I have the questions on a PDF, which you can find at www. ellementsgroup.com/moneyhoney if you want to print them off or share them with a friend.

Strut

FUN SHOE FACT: High heels for women are believed to have originated with Catherine de' Medici, a sixteenth-century Italian noblewoman who was short in stature and wanted to make a bigger impression when she arrived in France to marry the future King Henry. Go figure—a woman trying to impress a man.

SOLE QUOTE: "Cinderella is proof that a new pair of shoes can change your life." —Unknown

"The average woman falls in love seven times a year. Only six are with shoes."
—Kenneth Cole

SOUL QUOTE: "I hope you never find the words to describe love; I hope you never ruin what cannot be explained, trying to understand it." — Rachel Wolchin

"If someone ever tells you 'Don't fall in love, you might get hurt,' just tell them, 'Don't live, you might die.'" —Pinterest

FAB READS:

- *Smart Couples Finish Rich: 9 Steps to Creating a Rich Future* by David Bach

- *The Smart Cookies' Guide to Couples and Money: Earn More, Argue Less, Achieve the Life You Want ... Together* by Andrea Baxter, Angela Self, Katie Dunsworth, Robyn Gunn, and Sandra Hanna

- *Cold Hard Truth on Family, Kids and Money* by Kevin O'Leary

- *Make Every Man Want You* by Marie Forleo

SHOUT IT OUT: I love myself.

PUTTIN' ON THE SHOES:

🥿 If you are in a relationship that is "moneyogomous," look into cash flow planning! This tool has helped many couples achieve their goals together and manage day-to-day finances, thus creating equality even where there is income inequality. Go to www.ellementsgroup.com/cashflowplan to learn more.

🥿 Get into the conversation with your true love using these great MONEY HONEY questions at www.ellementsgroup.com/moneyhoney.

SHOEBOX NOTES:

🥿 Love is amazing, and being in love is possibly the best feeling in the world; however, relationships are hard work, so agree on a plan for your finances and how to handle day-to-day family/relationship operations. This will help you to keep your fights to something more important—like what movie to watch, or who ate the last chocolate cupcake, or what song you want to sing as a duet.

STRUT TUNES:

🥿 "Whose Bed Have Your Boots Been Under?" by Shania Twain

🥿 "Boots & Boys" by Ke$ha

🥿 "Shoes" by The Love Willows

🥿 "Dancing Shoes" by Green River Ordinance

7

Mary Janes

Children are the world's greatest assets, for in their innocent joy they are the greatest teachers to old, hardened hearts.

STYLE DESCRIPTION: A shoe for young girls that has a low heel, closed toe, and strap that buckles across the instep.

PROSPERITY DESCRIPTION: Small steps in planning for your children will bring a great wealth of knowledge for them and set an example for generations to come.

It was 1995. My first-ever board meeting was a complete disaster. It was a budget meeting at a beautiful, brand-new office complex. I was young, but not the youngest person in attendance. I remember being excited, dressing up and wearing my teal green blazer, looking all professional with my fancy pleather portfolio and pen, all ready to take notes; I felt very prepared for this meeting.

The thrill of sitting down at the beautiful oak table, the smell of stationary and dry erase markers, the feeling of sinking into the plush leather chairs: these distinct memories still get me going to this day. Budget spreadsheets, balance sheets, income statements, and goal-setting notes were carefully placed in front of each participant. There was an expense report with a staple in it; yes, there were that many pages involved in this detailed report that the document actually required a staple. The boss meant business.

Five minutes into the meeting I got kicked out by the president—CEO, Big Boss Man—and was sent to his corner office for a time out.

Thanks, Dad!

That's my claim to fame in this family: holding the record for being kicked out of the Annual Family Budget Meeting. And that's how the Loewen's rolled.

My dad had *everything* budgeted out. The questions posed to us children would be something along the lines of, "We need to cut out $4,000 from our expenses. We are broke. As you can see, family, the number at the bottom of page thirty-six of the budget report is written in the red!"

This was when I learned the colour red is bad. This reminds me of my first car, a red 1987 Honda Prelude, which had a front licence plate that said "'NTHERED." At seventeen, I knew what that meant. My dad even made me sign a new driver's contract; I didn't have a curfew, but my car did (parents 1, teenager 0).

Fallout from the meeting went something like this: my sister had to inventory the freezer, and her job was to make sure Mom did not buy extras or duplicate food at the grocery store (I should mention, as per my mom's disclaimer, that she is not unintelligent in the slightest; she just has a generational hoarding disorder). After the family meeting, we decided we could all go without Blockbuster (a movie rental place – how soon we forget our Friday night rituals), Mom's haircuts, and food for the dog for a total savings of $800, which wasn't quite the $4,000 my dad was hoping to cut out of the yearly budget). This led to my other sister crying when she thought our dog would die of starvation, which led to another family meeting to calm down and reassure my sister that we'd let Goldie, our bichon shih tzu, live. I was not privy to some of these decisions as I was, after all, stuck in the corner office. I'm sure the meeting outcomes were nothing like what my dad had intended, but we often laugh and bring up those meetings even to this day!

Okay, so my family experience may have been nothing like yours growing up, but I do have to take this time and say my parents did a very good job in attempting to instill in us children the basic financial principles. My mom was the bookkeeper—by my dad's design, I'm sure—and I remember many nights she'd stay up late "balancing the budget" on our Tandy computer. Yes, that was a long time ago, and I think our computer could do only two things: balance the budget and *Frogger*.

Between my mom's relentless logging of all receipts so my dad could produce lengthy spreadsheets and my dad's attempts at Sunday night family budget meetings, I think our parents taught us a lot about business and basic financial principles by setting that example for us. At the time, I know a lot of it was lost on us, but they kept at it, always setting a good example (some of which I still don't even follow), and somehow they turned out four half-decent children (yes, I am the ringleader of the four, being the eldest). Hey, I may not have attended the School of Hard Knocks, but I did attend the School of Dad (he never said I graduated ... I'm sure the diploma got lost in the mail—right, Dad?).

Childhood was one thing, but having your own kids just throws you for a loop. Really. No one tells you this parenting thing is going to be hard—challenging, at times—with the odd sprinkle of fun and delight. Okay, so it's not *that* bad at all, but again, they don't put warning labels on these things, and then you have to get them to pee and poo on their own, and then somehow find time to teach them about life.

All joking aside, I consider this one of the most important chapters in my book because you can be a total screw-up, and a total *financial* screw-up (and again, that's okay!), but teach your kids how to save and they'll save for a lifetime ... or better yet, teach your kids about the wonderful life-changing options financial freedom provides, and they'll change the world, cure diseases, invent more mind-blowing technologies, travel to galaxies unknown, solve world hunger, and make sure all the kids in this world are loved. Our kids will do that. It is our job as parents, guardians, educators, caregivers, and society, and it a job charged with the privilege of speaking into the lives of little people and encouraging them to fulfill their purposes and dreams. And as parents, we *want* our kids to have it better than we did, and we have the innate desire to advance humanity. It's part of our DNA; I'm sure of it.

When I was pregnant, I actually gave thought to what I was going to teach my kids about money and how I was going to make them successful, five-year-old day traders (like the baby that does his first trade on the e-trade commercial). However, all of this thinking occurred when I was pregnant (which was my first problem). That's when a parent's hopes and dreams form for their precious babies.

My five-year-old is an answer to a prayer. I prayed for a daughter, just like me—but be careful what you pray for. I love my "mini-me," but we are already butting heads, and I even got my first door slam last week. I obviously don't know anything, according to my five-year-old, and I hear it gets worse from here on in. And now I'm supposed to teach my child about money, when I can barely get them out the door to school in the morning on time?!

I ask my youngest, who is four, the following questions: "Sweetie, do you want Mommy to teach you about the stock market or microeconomics?" I get a blank stare.

"Mommy, can I just watch *Treehouse*?" she replies.

"Yes, honey, you can." And that ends that conversation, me deflated.

Choosing another tactic, I wait for teachable moments and start by setting an example. Yup, because clearly the lessons I had dreamt while pregnant of my perfectly behaved children went right out the window, lost somewhere between diapers and *SpongeBob*.

And if you 'feel' you are an old woman who lives in a shoe and has so many children you don't know what to do some days, here are some ideas.

So what can we do for our kids besides modelling good financial behaviour and talking about it? Here are three things I decided to do for mine as well as one great teaching tip:

1. RESPs
(Registered Education Savings Plans)

RESPs are a great way to save money for your child's education. There are two ways to hold the plans; individual and family. The administration of a family plan is easy if you have more than one child. For every $1 you put in, you get $0.20—up to a certain limit from the Canadian Government. That's right: there is a 20 percent return on your money for your child's education. Of course, the government doesn't do this willy-nilly, and there are many rules around these accounts (all of which your amazing financial coach will be able to explain for you, or a really good Google search). Always be mindful that when the government hands out funds, there are usually a lot of rules surrounding it. Nonetheless, this is still the best way to save for your child's education in Canada at the time of writing this – of course, that could change tomorrow.

2. Life Insurance/Critical Illness Insurance

Have you ever thought about getting critical illness insurance or life insurance on your babies?

Well, truth be told, as horrible as it seems to "profit" off your child's illness, or worse, death (yes, I've had this talk with many parents, many times!), it's something to consider for this simple reason: if your child had to be at the hospital every day or needed plenty of care for the foreseeable future, and you couldn't work (remember, disability is only if you can't work, not if your kids can't), how would that affect your family financially? If you are a single parent or if you are in a partnership that requires both of you to work to pay the bills every month, it's probably even more important. And if the worst-case scenario happens, then do you want the option to go back to work right away or not? Don't think of it as insuring your children; think of it more as insuring your job if you can't work.

Well, I found a way to make the "uneasiness" of buying critical illness and life insurance on your children less terrible. There is an insurance company that I use that offers a three-in-one policy; it's the best I have found, and, yes, I have these on my girls. I hunted for the best when I had my babies—so naturally, I share that with you! I'm quite passionate about these policies.

For whatever your selected face value, say $50,000 or $100,000 (very typical face amounts), if your child is diagnosed with a critical illness (the policy will pay out for a number of critical illnesses), or if your child dies prematurely, then it pays out the face amount upon death (and the last thing you want to be thinking about at a time like that is how you are going to pay your bills). So you get one or the other. However, if you are like me and you pray, hope, and expect your children to grow up healthy and happy, then guess what—twenty years later, you get all the premiums back! This is a lovely little lump sum of money you can gift to your child for university, perhaps a wedding, or a new home, or just keep it for your next shopping trip; after all, you just spent twenty years having to raise that child, so it's well-deserved shopping money! Also, it's important to note that after twenty years, the policy becomes "paid up," meaning you don't need to make any more payments every month. Then your child has a critical illness/life insurance policy for life, just in case he/she is uninsurable at the policy's twenty-year mark—so you don't have to cash it in for a refund of premium. That's like a four-in-one policy.

By the way, this is a great policy for grandparents who want to help to buy on their grandchildren, so if you can't afford the premiums, ask Oma or Baba or Nana to help.

My daughters will have seed money to get started in university and for whatever they need, be it a car or school accommodations. They will also have a paid-up policy that they can keep for the rest of their life if they are uninsurable, or they can cancel/collapse and take out the cash value and use it for something that's important to them (of course, they can cancel only after they have another policy approved and in place).

3. Non-Registered Accounts or "In Trust" Accounts

If you are maxing out your RESPs and have extra birthday and Christmas money kicking around, after you've bought new shoes for your growing child for the hundredth time ("oh, my sweet, endless money pits"—can I get an *amen,* sisters?), you can invest in an open or non-registered investment or savings account. It's nothing fancy; just a plain account you put after-tax dollars in, and you are taxed only on the growth. This type of account does have tax considerations depending on what type of investment your put your money in, but your advisor setting up the plan will be able to explain those.

It's important to note that you can't put money in a Tax Free Savings Account (TFSA) for anyone under eighteen. You can earmark money in your head for your kids in a TFSA if you aren't using all the room in yours for you, but it can't be legally in the name of the child.

You can also go to the bank and set up a savings account for your kids and get them their own card and teach them how to use it. I remember doing this in Grade 4, when I opened up my first RBC Leo Lion Savers account. I remember getting to use the ATM—fun! Kids love that stuff.

On a side note, there will be times you aren't contributing to your children's future, and that's okay. I can honestly say I stopped all contributions to RRSP, RESP, and whatever else for at least six months one time when life had its crazy unplanned turns or hard times. I didn't know what money was going to be coming in, and I needed to make sure I had enough money to live on. And again, that's okay! Life happens; just make a plan to get back on track when you can. We all have times in our life where things don't go as planned.

Here's where the grandparents' contribution comes in. If you are already maxing out your RESPs (which honestly, according to the government, very few people do), then you can get the grandparents to help invest into that account, or they can also do a non-registered "in-trust" account for your child. It's best if any non-registered accounts are invested in equities (also known as stocks or common shares), so the capital gains are taxed in the hands of the child. However, if you can't stomach that, then put the money in an investment that you feel suits your risk tolerance; the contributor may just be stuck paying tax on the growth. However, unless you are taking large sums of money, usually this isn't a problem for grandparents wanting to tuck away a few bucks every year for their grandchildren. Grandparents can also purchase the life insurance policies on the grandchild, as mentioned above.

Bonus tip: As for teaching your kids about money, I think the greatest thing you can do is include them in decisions, shopping trips, and conversations about how much things cost, especially when they are learning to count. And make it fun, because it is! There are those amazing little piggybanks that some brilliant person created that are labeled Give, Save, and Spend. Teach your kids to give 10 percent away, save 10 percent, and the rest they can spend. Or whatever percentage works. The idea is to get them in the habit to give, save, and spend and thus to begin growing that awareness in them.

It's important to educate your kids about money while they are young, teaching them and providing tools so they can have a good start. There are even great iPad apps you can play with. Even if you are dead set against giving your kids a penny—which is absolutely okay—please make sure they get some 'money sense' from you, and please teach them through the mistakes that you made by sharing (you don't need to share details to share examples). Oh, yes, you know they will go out and make their own mistakes, but they'll have the voice of someone who cares about them in their head.

Here's some final food for thought: the truth is, if you do save money and education funds and get your child their own insurance policy for the future, anything you do for your child, they will grow up and notice that, and they will notice your actions, and actions speak louder than just telling them to save. Even more so, save money and set aside money for *your* future. That will be one powerful lesson you can show your kids. Not only is it wise for yourself, but it is also a small action your children will notice and pick up on. The apples don't fall far from the tree for good reason; your kids will grow up to be just like you, all the good parts and all the bad. So let your kids know about the family financial situation, and the insurance that you have, and the benefits of savings.

I wrote an awesome quick and easy financial guide to parenthood that you can check out at www.ellementsgroup.com/get-the-guide.

FUN SHOE FACT: The best-selling shoe size is 8.5 for women and 10.5 for men. These are up a full size from thirty years ago, according to the National Shoe Retailers Association in a *Chicago Tribune* article in 2011.

SOLE QUOTE: "Give a girl the right shoes, and she can conquer the world." —Marilyn Monroe

SOUL QUOTE: "If you want your children to turn out well, spend twice as much time with them, and half as much money." —Abigail Van Buren

"You were born an original. Don't die a copy." —John Mason

FAB READS:

ᄂ   *The Prosperity Factor for Kids* by Kelley Keehn

ᄂ   *Smart Money Smart Kids* by Rachel Cruze and Dave Ramsey

SHOUT IT OUT: I love others unconditionally.

PUTTIN' ON THE SHOES:

ᄂ   Be conscious of the money "stories," values, habits, and words you speak around your children.

ᄂ   Make money a game.

ᄂ   If you want to have fun, try making a kid's net worth statement (create a new name) and watch it grow.

ᄂ   Get your FREE copy of "The Ultimate Quick Financial Guide to Parenthood: What Every Parent Must Know Financially" at www. ellementsgroup.com/get-the-guide

Shoebox Notes:

ᄂ   Have fun and make money management a learning game with your children. Be open about finances and how things work.

ᄂ   Help your kids get on the right track financially: help them save, start an RESP, or other savings accounts.

ᄂ   If insurance makes sense for your family, get your child's policies started.

ᄂ   Teach your children about a company, and if they want to learn more, start a practice online trading account. Almost all online trading companies offer free practice trading accounts, such as RBC Direct Investing or Scotia iTrade.

Strut Tunes (for kids):

ᄂ   "Jump Up!" by Imagination Movers

ᄂ   "7-8-9" by Barenaked Ladies

ᄂ   "Goody Two Shoes" by Adam Ant

ᄂ   "Love Is an Open Door" by Kristen Bell and Santino Fontana

8

Oxfords

*Find something you're passionate about and keep
tremendously interested in it.*
—Julia Child

*Your mind and body will be around a lot longer than
those expensive shoes you just bought—invest in
yourself.*
—Lisa Elle

STYLE DESCRIPTION: A type of laced-up shoe over the instep with a low heel.

PROSPERITY DESCRIPTION: Investment in people and yourself will be the greatest investment of all time.

I went to Oxford. Once. The town, that is, where the big university is situated. These were the crazy things my girlfriend and I did backpacking around Europe; we'd go places just to say we went. And Oxford was no exception. I mean, really, it's such a cool thing to say you went to Oxford.... Okay, perhaps it's cooler to say, "I studied at Oxford," but "went" works for me. My family and friends still bug me, because I came back from my year abroad and made a point to mention that "the air is cleaner in Europe." That's still the running joke, although now, seventeen years later, Canadian air is quite incredible.

The old adage, Parkinson's Law, says that "work expands so as to fill the time available for its completion."

You think you don't have time to learn—I mean, who has time for anything these days? You just need to create that space, and amazing things open up. Be a lifelong learner. Not only will you learn and begin to ignite new ideas, but also the side effect is you begin to sound smart at cocktail parties. Learn to love to read, and read everything you can get your hands on in your favourite subject.

I am the first to know traditional education does not make you wealthy; it may provide for a better paying job, but some of the most successful people I know barely made it out of high school. So we need to not make traditional education paths the be-all and end-all. Learning comes in many forms, and many specialized fields have no classrooms, just the classroom of life. Even if you didn't go to university because you took a year off after high school, married your high-school sweetheart, and popped out a litter of children, that's awesome. Perhaps now your kids are a bit older and you can move on, find something you're passionate about, make it your investment, and learn everything there is to know about what it is you love. There are no shortages of experts in this world. And, according to my girl, Marie Forleo, "Learners are earners, so keep going, girl!"[18]

Angela Lee Duckworth, in her TED Talk "The Key to Success? Grit," says that "grit, being the most significant predictor of success,

18 Marie Forleo, "When Inspiration Backfires," *readable*, accessed April 6, 2016, http://www.allreadable.com/e22a5LY6.

is passion and perseverance for very long-term goals. Grit is having stamina. Grit is sticking with your future, day in, day out."[19] Failure is not a permanent condition, although somehow we can trick ourselves into believing that.

Learning puts us in a place of vulnerability, to which the best definition I have found on this word is "To voluntarily place yourself in a situation that could bring pain for the sake of a larger purpose" (dictionary). It's really just about putting yourself out there. Education, in its simplest form, is admitting you don't know something but having the desire to follow through in acquiring that knowledge. But there's a part two to that equation, which is not as widely talked about, and it's in the sharing of that knowledge once attained; it's the value add, and that's what makes the world tick and things happen. It's through the sharing of experience, connection, and teaching that we bring about products, services, and value added to our world, and I would even go as far to add love to that list. We want to hold our education as our trophy of pride. I'm no exception. We worked hard for those capital letters beside our name, and the truth of the matter is we will never be able to impact the world and create positive changes by clinging to those or the strength of our résumé.

I mentioned how inadequate I feel writing this book. I feel I need another three more financial designations behind my name before I can even *begin* this conversation or for anyone to really take me seriously. I also feel I need a few more grey hairs and loads more life experience to come out with something that will "really make an impact." But I don't. And I'm gonna screw up and fail, whether that's now or when I'm sixty. So I send my "fear shoes," and my "unsmart shoes" to the dump. No one needs to wear those at any time, and I know we all have nasty old pairs of shoes like that in our shoe closets. Maybe it's time for a spring cleaning.

19 Angela Lee Duckworth, "The Key to Success? Grit," Ted Talk, *Ted Talks Education*, April 2013, https://www.ted.com/talks/ angela_lee_duckworth_the_key_to_success_grit?language=en.

Creating Vs. Consuming

In life, we are either creating or consuming. Our success lies in the creating. It makes sense. Consuming acts—such as reading, watching TV, eating, or spending countless hours on the newsfeed on your many social media sites—are sure not to bring you success in any area of your life. Consuming is kicking back and letting life entertain you.

I think a ratio of creating versus consuming should be 2:1, meaning we should aim for twice as much creating versus consuming. Which makes sense; typically, in your day job, whatever it may be, you are creating, whether you are doing laundry, cooking, sending emails, making phone calls, connecting, or writing. These are all creating tasks. You know the days where all you do is stay in your PJs and drown yourself in *You've Got Mail* and *Sleepless in Seattle* along with two bags of Lays chips and three candy bars? (I have *never* done this myself, and there's no proof, either.) Those pity-party days are examples of consumption days. Limiting these is always best.

Another way to look at it is earning versus spending. When you are earning, you are adding value and inevitably creating, and when you are spending, you are consuming. Successful people spend even less time consuming. Even God's ratio is 6:1—six days creating, and one day to kick back and enjoy.

Here's another thing: learning takes place in both the creating and consuming arenas. To learn, you read and listen to teachers, lectures, or bosses. Then I observed my kids build a fort in the living room. Kids naturally have a healthy creating-versus-consuming ratio built into them.

We all learn through creating—through trial and error. I learn while I write, and even when I talk, I come to realizations at times. When I look up something, when I am writing or inspiration strikes and guides me, or when I am talking through something and new ideas emerge, or I piece something together through brainstorming and something just clicks—that's all learning.

I think, for the most part, balance comes naturally to us. After all, how many Meg Ryan movies can you watch in a row before you want to get off your butt? Okay, this is a bad example for me—I could do that all day!

We were built to create. However, I fear that over the last few decades, society in general has become more complacent with creating, probably due to new technology, and not natural human behaviour. I don't think human nature has changed. We always choose the path of least resistance and survival. If you gave a caveman an iPhone, I bet he'd spend all day on Facebook and order all his hunting gear off Amazon, too! I think our ratio has shifted from centuries ago, where creating was what you had to do to survive, and of course it still is, but I think our ratio is becoming consumption-heavy.

This whole creating-versus-consuming thing is something worth considering in your own life. If you keep your creating/earning side in full force, you will be amazed at how much you can accomplish. I also will tell you that all engaged, passionate people I know are also financially successful.

Everyone has the same twenty-four hours a day. Consuming is important, too! It's how we rest, rejuvenate, and relax just long enough to get our next great idea, and off we go, back to creating again.

Next time you are exercising or at work organizing, replying, quoting, or sharing, take pride in your creating. We aren't all traditional artists, but we *are* all artists of creation in our own ways.

In regards to your life right now, if there is something you are passionate to learn about, or a course you wish you could take, what is holding you back? Is it any of the main culprits, such as the lack of time, no money, laziness, lack of passion, or too much fear?

Funny thing: I actually knew I wanted to be a financial advisor since I was eighteen. I had a cute boyfriend that hooked me up with his financial advisor, Vicki. I met Vicki and just wanted to do what she was doing. I started investing and learning.

Education is a great thing. I plan on still taking courses when I'm eighty years old and have so many letters beside my name I could rewrite the alphabet. But achieving your dreams is not *just* about education. I think education is the catalyst.

"Learning leads to knowledge, knowledge breeds confidence, and when confidence is coupled with faith, this leads to passion." —Lisa Elle

Investing in yourself has to be top priority.

"When you have good shoes on, it's easier for you to help carry others." —Lisa Elle

Investing in yourself also means investing in your own business, if that's something that interests you. I think everyone should have their own business or part-time business in some way, shape, or form; the tax benefits alone make it worthwhile. This is something you can discuss further with your accountant or financial advisor to get you set up if you don't know where to start on the money end, and if you don't know what you want to do, a life coach or business coach is a great resource to help you figure out what you want to do with your life. I do know having your own business is not for everyone.

"When talking about net worth statements, assets, and liabilities, you need to remember that *you* are your greatest asset, with your knowledge and what you do with that knowledge. Your greatest liability is to not know this." —Lisa Elle

FUN SHOE FACT: Oxford shoes were actually named after Oxford University in the 1800s and are known as a more formal lace-up shoe.

SOLE QUOTE: "When you have good shoes on, it's easier to help carry others." —Lisa Elle

SOUL QUOTE: "Do what you love, and you'll never work a day in your life." —Confucius

FAB READS:

➴ *The Cashflow Quadrant: Rich Dad's Guide to Financial Freed*om by Robert Kiyosaki and Sharon Lechter

➴ *Rich Dad, Poor Da*d by Robert Kiyosaki and Sharon Lechter

➴ *The War of Art: Break Through the Blocks and Win Your Inner Creative Battle*s by Steven Pressfield

➴ *Turning Pro: Tap Your Inner Power and Create Your Life's Wor*k by Steven Pressfield

SHOUT IT OUT: I have all the knowledge of the universe available to me.

PUTTIN' ON THE SHOES:

➴ Enroll yourself into something that brings you joy! A class, a workshop, a seminar, a course, a program: this will give you purpose and lead you to your purpose if you haven't figured out what that purpose is.

➴ Find fabulous free resources, blogs, and gurus in your favourite subjects to follow online.

SHOEBOX NOTES:

➴ Investing in yourself should be your number-one priority—you are your own greatest asset.

➴ Education is always important (formal or informal); the moment you stop learning or think you know it all, you start dying.

➴ Investing in yourself also means investing in your own business.

STRUT TUNES:

➴ "Perfect Day" by Hoku

➴ "Boogie Shoes" by K.C. and the Sunshine Band

➴ "Shut Up and Dance" by Walk the Moon

➴ "Girl on Fire" by Alicia Keys

9
Penny Loafers

They say death and taxes are the only certain things in life—but so are laundry and dishes.

The only difference between death and taxes is death doesn't get worse every time Congress meets.
—Will Rogers

STYLE DESCRIPTION: A casual leather sole with a decorative slotted leather strip over the upper part, in which a coin may be placed.

PROSPERITY DESCRIPTION: Taxes are inevitable—you are playing the game already. The problem is the fact that most don't know the rules, or they don't know they're even on the field.

I **dreaded writing** How the hell am I going to take the eye-poking-pulling-teeth-boring-as-(insert profanity of choice) subject of *tax*, explain some basics, and make it somewhat enjoyable to read? There's a short answer here: I'm not. Taxes are worse than death; death is a taxable event.

Hence, this chapter is crucial—crucial to investing and so crucial to most of your financial decisions. It's *so* crucial that I asked my friends about it in a questionnaire. The inquiries were, "Do you know the difference between a tax credit and a tax deduction?" and "Do you know the difference between tax evasion and tax avoidance?" Almost all my wine-drinking girlfriends responded with, "More wine please." Somehow, the conversation immediately went on to *far* more important things, such as "Who is Kim Kardashian's baby daddy, really?" and "Why does bread mould?" These are truly fascinating conversation topics to enjoy over a glass of fermented grapes— definitely more fascinating than examining where you would rather have a million dollars: in a TFSA or an RRSP (P.S. Of course you want a million dollars in your *tax*-free savings account....).

And to further this wretched talk, I am not an accountant. I truly disliked accounting in college. It was all about man-made rules (and still is, the last I checked) that made no sense most of the time (okay— all the time), and the rules change all the time. In fact, the Income Tax Act of Canada changes every year. Although I'm not an accountant (probably because they would own only one pair of shoes—*penny loafers!* Oh ya!), as a financial planner, I need to be well versed in the tax rules. And as a person who files taxes, it is so important to know what's going on. (As a side note: taxes are another reason having a good accountant and a good financial planner are important—and it's best if they can work together on your plan.)

My next chapter is on investments, which is the Vegas of finance: flashy, fun, exciting, and daring. Tax, on the other hand, is the Athol. Athol, Idaho. Really, this place exists, and I've been there. A small town in the middle of nowhere Idaho. It's not fun. It's not exciting like Vegas. But on your drive to Vegas, you will need to pass through Athol first, same as investing. If you want the fun, shiny, sparkling part of business and investing, then you need to pass through the Athol of tax. Tax can be painful. It's just how it is. (Okay, I'd like to give a *huge* apology to my accountant sweeties reading this. We love you! *Really, we do! MUAH!*) And for my non-numbers friends, don't even try to book your root canal right now ... finish the next two pages.

It's so crazy, the world in which we live—but regardless of where you live, you will most likely need to file a tax return, and because of that simple fact, you are automatically playing a game in the world of money regardless of whether you know the rules of the game. If you don't know the rules of this game, then may I suggest your opponent could very well be winning? And on that note, may I also suggest that no matter who you are, your opponent is a lot bigger and, combined, a lot smarter than you? That's not to say you can't learn a few quick tricks to stay a few steps ahead of your opponent. So put on your penny loafers, and we will talk a quick game of taxes—the must-knows, in my opinion.

There are many different types of tax in Canada, and before you know some of the rules, let me paint a picture for those that really don't think they pay any tax—because I know you are out there. For starters, everyone pays our Goods & Service Tax (GST), which currently sits at 5 percent across Canada, and then you have your provincial sales tax, which varies from province to province.

We also earn income. Income is typically most of the money we earn. It is taxed fully at the highest rates, depending on your level of income. In Canada, we have other taxes to include. This is a very short list, but never forget the property tax you are paying (even if you rent, your rent is covering the property tax on the home you live in), and I've already mentioned sales taxes, but there's also tobacco, liquor, amusement, automobile, and gas taxes, and let's not forget import duties on many of the items we consume.

On average, 41.5 percent of the average family's income goes to pay one form of tax or another, the largest being income taxes. The other taxes being inescapable, but what we can do is find ways to lessen our income taxes.[20]

---

20 Charles Lammam and Milagros Palacios, "How Much Taxes Do Canadians Really Pay?", *Troy Media*, April 27, 2012, http://www.troymedia.com/2012/04/27/how-much-tax-do-canadians-really-pay/.

Suggestion #1: Move to Alberta. Okay, I joke—and this is a long-running joke I have between many friends and family members who live in Ontario and BC because Alberta used to be the "cheapest" tax province to live in. However, it is a valid point to note money does flow to where it gets taxed the least. We can move freely—our businesses, too—and naturally, money will flow to the place where the least resistance is. That's just something to keep in the back of your head when investing, and as a Canadian citizen. Okay, so you may not move to another province just to save a few tax dollars, however, when you're making millions or big businesses that do, they definitely move to where money is cheapest or where tax incentives are.

There are three ways investments get taxed in Canada: interest, dividends, and capital gains. Interest income is added to your income and thus taxed at the highest rates (the same rate as your income), whereas eligible dividends and capital gains tax are more preferred, hence you pay less tax. Foreign Investments, if you own any, are also taxed at your highest rate (same rate as your income), although there are tax treaties with certain countries to avoid double taxation, and you'll need a good accountant who is well versed in that country's tax rulings as well.

Here is a bird's-eye simplified view of some of the possible slips you may see come your way at tax time. A T4 or T4A slip from your employer at tax time from the salary, wages, bonuses, employment commissions, vacation pay, etc., will show all the income you need to report and pay income tax on. T3 slips or T3 Statement of Trust Income is usually for income received from a trust or non-registered mutual fund trust. T5 slips indicate how much investment income you earned from dividends, royalties, investments, interest from bank accounts, insurance policies, etc. You probably won't be receiving a T5 slip if you earned under $50 from any one institution. Capital gains (or capital losses) you typically need to keep track of yourself through good record keeping. You may get some statements for investments you sold, however, they really are voluntary disclosures, so another reason keeping good records is so important.

This chart shows the least and most preferable ways to get taxed in Canada at the time of writing this—and this chart will change from time to time, so again, consult your accountant:

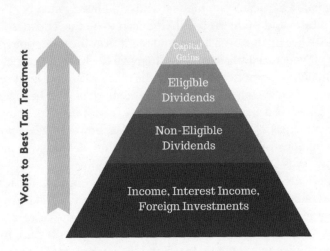

So those are the ways dollars get taxed in Canada. Now, we need to know how those dollars fit into our everyday lives and how different types of accounts get taxed.

When surveying my friends and asking this question—specifically, "Do you know how much tax you paid last year, or the percentage of tax you paid?"—100 percent of my friends said "No." Again, perhaps wine was involved, but I really don't think that has any bearing on the quality of this specific research question, as I'm very sure 97 percent of women don't care—sadly, I'm in the same camp. (And by now you know I had to feed my friends a lot of wine to get them to answer any of my boring questions! Many bottles were sacrificed in the making of this book.)

I can't tell you how many times I've had clients say to me something along the line of (and I'm sure many other advisors, tax professionals, etc., will have a laugh at the recognition of this): "I think I want mutual funds instead of RRSPs," or "My investment account is doing horribly; can I switch it to an RRSP? Will that do better?"

Okay—you didn't see the humour in that? It's funny because they are talking about two different things, one being the type of account, and the other being what's held in the account or the type of investment.

So many of my beautiful dears get stuck on this every time. So now for a shoe analogy: You have money to burn and there's a party tonight, and you need new shoes for your sexy LBD (little black dress). So you go shopping. But before you buy your dream shoes, you have to pick a bag to take with you while shopping, because once you buy your shoes they will need to go into a bag so you can accomplish your goal of getting the shoes home safe so you can wear them to tonight's party—goal accomplished. (The assumption is we are very eco-friendly-recycling people and we bring our own bags!) So while at home, you look around, and all you have is your designer Coach bag and a plastic Safeway grocery shopping bag with holes in it. Both are bags, and both will probably help you achieve your goal, which is to bring home your dream shoes. However, the Coach bag will probably bring your shoes home safely without damage from the elements, while your holey Safeway bag may not get the job done and rip while you're walking down the street. However, they are two bags, and they have the same function—to store shoes. And let's not kid ourselves: our dream shoes need to be in the right bag because we just spent today's life savings on these shoes.

In the analogy, our shoes are the investments, such as stocks, bonds, mutual funds, ETFs, GICs (Guaranteed Investment Certificates), gold, silver—to name a few. Our bags are the types of accounts we can hold these investments in, such as non-registered or open, RRSP (Registered Retirement Savings Plan), TFSA, RESP (Registered Education Savings Plan), LIRA (Locked In Retirement Account), pensions, and, when the time comes, RRIF (Registered Retirement Income Fund), Life Income Fund (LIF), annuities, and the list goes on. So you want your investment (the shoes) to be held in the right type of account (the bag) for tax purposes. The wrong type of account (or that holey bag) could really cost you.

We also need to know what the difference is between a tax deduction and a tax credit. Tax deduction will reduce your taxable income right off the top from a qualifying expense, and for most employees, the most common is an RRSP purchase. If you have your own business, then the deductions are almost endless. This is one of the greatest tax advantages you can take advantage of (more on this later).

Tax credits are deducted directly from the tax liability or the tax you owe. Common tax credits include: spouse or common-law partner, children, medical expense, children's fitness, children's art, caregiver, age credit, public transport, charitable donations, etc., etc.

As far as tax treatment goes, the main thing I can teach you before you really need to speak with your advisor is the following: RRSPs are 100 percent tax deductible, as they are 100 percent taxable income to you when you withdraw them (and when you withdraw them, depending on the amount, the CRA takes a withholding tax of 10, 20, or 30 percent right off the top—trust me when I say the taxman always gets his fair share!), and you have to rectify that on your tax return and could end up owing more come filing time.

TFSAs have no tax incentive when you put money in. You are putting in after-tax dollars, or the money you've already paid tax on. The bonus is when you need money from your TFSA, there is no tax on the growth. Also, to boot, if you lose money, you don't get a tax loss to offset your gains, as you would in a non-registered or open account.

A non-registered or open account—or even your chequing or savings accounts—are all with dollars you've typically paid tax on already.

Taxes filing deadlines in Canada are on April 30 for most individuals and June 15 for self-employed people, however, the tax owing is still due on April 30 every year for tax owed on the previous calendar year.

And, yes, you can Google all this information, and I encourage you to search it out and take warning. With taxes, there are too many moving parts, and at the end of the day, a professional tax accountant, a professional tax advisor, or a professional financial advisor can and should ask all the right questions to get you to pay the least amount of tax.

In Canada, hire a CPA (Certified Professional Accountant) to help you steer the ever-changing waters of our complex tax code—period. I don't recommend doing your own taxes, unless you are a wiz and have only a few slips to deal with at the end of the year. For anyone with a more complex tax situation, I absolutely recommend hiring a tax professional (just don't tell him how many pairs of shoes you bought this year—that might freak him out!). The cost will be well worth it to you over the years.

You really shouldn't be too excited about your tax return (if you are lucky to get one); it's just money that was yours already being returned to you.

I found this poem, and it's basically the reason this eye-poking chapter had to be included. You will be taxed, so it's better to know what this is all about.

TAX POEM

Tax his land, tax his wage,
Tax his bed in which he lays.
Tax his tractor, tax his mule,
Teach him taxes is the rule.
Tax his cow, tax his goat,
Tax his pants, tax his coat.
Tax his ties, tax his shirts,
Tax his work, tax his dirt.
Tax his chew, tax his smoke,
Teach him taxes are no joke.
Tax his car, tax his ass
Tax the roads he must pass.
Tax his tobacco, tax his drink,
Tax him if he tries to think.
Tax his booze, tax his beers,
If he cries, tax his tears.
Tax his bills, tax his gas,
Tax his notes, tax his cash.
Tax him good and let him know
That after taxes, he has no dough.
If he hollers, tax him more,
Tax him until he's good and sore.

Tax his coffin, tax his grave,
Tax the sod in which he lays.
Put these words upon his tomb,
"Taxes drove me to my doom!"
And when he's gone, we won't relax,
We'll still be after the inheritance TAX!

—Author unknown[21]

FUN SHOE FACT: Do you know the import duties and taxes vary for the type of shoe, as well as the materials the shoe is made out of? Just go to www.dutycalculator.com and you will be amazed. Why does a boy's plastic slipper have 17 percent tax and a woman's loafer 11 percent? These are things that make you go "hmmm...."

SOLE QUOTE: "Money can't buy happiness, but it can buy shoes, which is essentially the same thing." —Unknown

SOUL QUOTE: "Some cause happiness wherever they go; others whenever they go." —Oscar Wilde

FAB READS:

 101 Tax Secrets for Canadians: Smart Strategies that Can Save You Thousands by Tim Cestnick

---

21 Unknown author quoted in Harry Choron and Sandy Choron, *Money: Everything You Never Knew About Your Favourite Thing to Find, Covet, Save and Spend* (San Francisco: Chronicle Books, 2011), 46.

Strut

- *78 Tax Tips for Canadians For Dummies* by Christie Henderson, Brian Quinlan, and Suzy Schultz

- *The Wealthy Barber: The Common Sense Guide to Successful Financial Planning* by David Chilton

- *The Wealthy Barber Returns* by David Chilton (I have *a huge* celebrity crush on him ... *sigh*!)

SHOUT IT OUT: I teach and share with others.

PUTTIN' ON THE SHOES:

- Get *a great* accountant! Hire a CPA (Certified Professional Accountant) in Canada! This will save you money over the year and help you utilize all credits and deductions available to you.

- Talk with your accountant and CFP and get them both on board with your goals.

SHOEBOX NOTES:

- Learn the rules of the tax game so you can *win*—because you are forced to play this game anyways!

- Tax law, tax code, tax rules—*anything* tax-related *will* always change, so you need to hire a good accountant or stay abreast of the changes. (I've always wanted to say "abreast"! Haha ... Yes, I am a total nine-year-old at times.)

- If you learn nothing else from this chapter, chew on this: "The point to remember is that what the government gives it must first take away." —John S. Coleman

STRUT TUNES:

- Sorry, there are no happy songs about taxes. However, there is a bottle of wine (whine?) with your name on it.

10

Running Shoes

Get moving (running) in the right direction.

STYLE DESCRIPTION: Athletic footwear primarily designed for sports or other forms of physical exercise.

PROSPERITY DESCRIPTION: Investing with knowledge mixed with intention and topped with a great plan will get you your desired outcome.

This was honestly one of my hardest chapters to condense down. I have so much to say and so many amazing financial gurus that have poured into my life that I want to share as many fundamentals that I can, without boring you to death! So I'm going to **bold** the key points as we walk through the twisty roads in my brain on this fun topic of investing.

But before I do, I want to say this chapter is geared toward my accumulators. As stated before, I categorize my clients in two categories: the accumulation phase and the distribution phase. Just to be clear, this chapter is geared for my gals that are growing their assets and not needing what they have built up to draw upon in later years. Although many points apply to both, I just wanted to clarify that.

Key point 1: Don't think the investment world is scary, because it's not. It sounds scary because people get paid millions and billions of dollars to make it sound complicated and scarier than it really is. After all, if it was uncomplicated and simple, they'd all be out of jobs!

It's taken me years to learn all the lingo, acronyms, and terminology, and to be able to sit down and watch *Business News Network* (*BNN*) for more than ten seconds. Sadly, *BNN* went from Greek to fluent English for me, and I actually enjoy watching most segments of *BNN* and talk radio, which makes me feel old.

After sitting in the car with my dad as a teenager listening to talk radio, I vowed never to listen to talk radio because it was so boring and we should all be listening to music all the time. Now, I attend Audio University every time I drive somewhere, with the odd nostalgic song sneaking its way in once in a while. Somewhere in the last eighteen years, I changed from music to talk radio.

And there again comes my good yet annoying friend: *change*.

Key point 2: The financial world is always changing. Nothing stays the same today for longer than one second. Information travels instantaneously, so when it comes to investing, just remember by the time you know, so does everybody else. You are last to the party. Markets in general are very efficient, and one of the goals is to exploit the inefficiencies and take advantage of them. Also keep in mind that news is built into the market and reflected today, even if it's news about something that will happen later down the road. I heard once that most market swings are half rational and half irrational. I believe that. To every 10 percent drop or rise in the market of any kind, half of the people thought it out carefully and methodically, and half just jumped on the bandwagon.

So why build your life worrying about something or focusing on something you can't control? No one can really understand or predict with any absolute certainty. First of all, you need to know that what matters in the end isn't what changes, such as technology, institutions, governments, markets, investment products, and social media. What matters is what actions and intentions you create—creating a life you love, practicing integrity, diversification, service, and love, and making the world a better place by fulfilling your unique purpose here.

Keeping your mind off the past is a very difficult thing in general terms. We bring our past experiences into our future, and although our past may serve as warnings, or lessons, all too often there is a grey area; not everything is absolute. Okay, so you lost money in your RRSP, and now you think all mutual funds are bad. That's like saying all people are bad, and you know that's not true. Don't extrapolate your most recent experiences to your expectation of tomorrow. When you do that, you lose your long-term perspective and get lost in the past. It's over, and what's important is the now. So be open-minded (humility is needed) enough to learn and want to know. When you say "never," you are closing your mind off to the opportunities that exist for you to make your dreams a reality. The press, social media, news, your great aunt Bertha, or your dad (who knows everything)—they are the noise, or "the great expositors of everything that happened yesterday." Trust me! The trick is to separate the noise from where money is flowing, and then figuring out supply-and-demand trends. Again, people adding value to other people is all that really matters. That is how money is made and money is kept.

I want to make investing less scary for you, and tell you what is *essential*—not what really won't matter in fifteen years or two minutes from now. I covered risk in Pair 2, "Flip-Flops," so remember the real risks.

Key point 3: The big risk is not doing any financial planning, saving or investing! After surveying my friends—and all my friends are smart women, by the way, and highly educated—I found 80 percent of my own friends find investing intimidating (a fear of the unknown) and would just rather play it safe, yet they know they need to do something.

The tricky part is sorting through mountains of information out there—what's real, what's hype, what's fake. This is where most of us—in fact, all of us—get stuck, because we will never know the truth (because the truth to one person may not be the truth to another, and that is a whole other book!) So what we have to do is go with best guesses, hypotheses, take asymmetric information, form our own conclusions, and take financial action with them.

But wait! Who has time for this? I sure don't! I am building my business, raising kids, and making a difference with the gifts I was given. I don't have the time to sit at a computer all day and intimately dissect information. I'm guessing you don't, either.

I want you to know *I am not a money manager*. I gather assets, allocate them, direct them, raise capital for private offerings, but I do not directly manage them, nor do I pretend to, nor do I want to! I'm not going to pretend to do a job that requires a FULL team of analysts; however, the analysts don't sit around and have time to sell the investments or bring them to market or gather money, so they work with us financial advisors to bring the best ideas to the market to you.

For most people with jobs or businesses, they don't have time to manage their own funds, yet for some reason professional money managers always get a bad rap the second you "feel" you lose money. (I say "feel," because until you actually sell off your position, all losses are not crystallized.) Unless someone is swindling you and is a criminal, most are just doing the best they can with the tools they have. And on that note....

Key point 4: We are all just doing our best with the tools and gifts we were given. So we hire stockbrokers, mutual fund managers, private equity firms, and independent advisors, and they decide on the best route for the money, whether it be in cash, bonds, stocks, resources, etc. If you are independently wealthy or a large company, you still have advisors manage your money; you just hire them on your payroll, and that's their job—to manage the excess of your corporation. So don't feel like you need to do it on your own. Most people and most businesses have some form of professional money manager to help them maintain and grow their balance sheets. We all have our own unique gifts, and we don't all have to be good at all things.

As far as investor satisfaction goes, there was a study done in the past (although I can't remember where I heard this,, but I know it to be true!) on a group of people who obtained the rate of return they wanted in their portfolio; whatever it was they wanted, they got. One would think all the people would be happy, but you know that's not the case. It's the ultimate investor psychology: greed. When we hit our goals, we so often want more. If we don't hit our goals, we want more. We just always want *more*, period. So when it comes to your investments, or your financial status in this world, just remember today is perfect and where you need to be. Take some advice from Socrates if you are in the "wishing you had more" category: "He who is not contented with what he has, would not be contented with what he would like to have."

Key point 5: We create the value as humans, and as humans we also place the meaning on what's valuable and what's not. Any investment is only as good as what the people around it think it is worth, or what value it has to them. It's all perceived value. Actual market value is the price someone will actually pay for something. Take your home, for example. You need to keep warm, and you need a place over your head. So on average, your house is worth more than your car. But we, as society, created that, and we created the meaning behind the value the house adds. It is funny; we create the value of things, but things at the end of the day are just things. Why do we value diamonds over, say, Styrofoam? Imagine if everyone thought Styrofoam was special—crazy, right? Everything at some point in time was a raw material from our lovely planet Earth that man converted/combined/ transformed into something else, which our blood, sweat, and tears went into, and we gave it value.

I tell you this because nothing is intimidating about the investment world; it's just something else that we give meaning to.

The stock markets came together like any market did, as a place of trade. And that's all it really is.

Key point 6: For every transaction, there is a buyer and a seller. If there is no buyer, then the seller is out of luck, and whatever he is selling is worthless. Remember the tulip and bulb craze of 1637 in Holland? (It's okay if you don't—you can Google it!)

In her fantastic book *Practically Investing*, Coreen T. Sol sums this phenomenon up so nicely that I couldn't have said it better myself:

> For every transaction, there is someone willing to buy and someone willing to sell at an agreed price, both believing that it's good value and that the counterparty is a little crazy. [...] That's what's fun about this. The differences of opinion are what keep markets humming and prices continually adjusting to find the fair value. It's been said that it's only a fair trade when both parties consider the other to have received the better deal.[22]

Your financial advisor is a person to keep you accountable to your plan and the goals you set out for yourself. Everyone needs one; even myself. I could even argue myself more than others. I have a shoe problem ... remember? So it's like a doctor—they don't treat themselves, and when they do, they end up in rehab clinics.

Key point 7: Here's another little great tidbit. Make sure you ask your advisor whether he holds the funds he's recommending, or whether all the funds he recommends the fund managers have to invest their own assets in them. Also, ask how the portfolio managers get compensated. Some managers get compensated only if they post positive returns, or a bulk of their compensation is for creating positive returns over many years, not just based on the flavour of the day. It's so important to ask these questions. I love investing with portfolio managers who have all their money in their own funds and who get compensated on producing fantastic results

---

22 Coreen T. Sol, *Practically Investing: Smart Investment Techniques Your Neighbour Doesn't Know About* (Bloomington, IN: iUniverse, 2014), 3.

over many years because they have their skin in the game. Also, they will typically still be investing for you for years to come and not just jump ship on your portfolio.

On that note, most investments are not bad; it's the human behaviour around them that makes them bad. We sell out of fear and buy in euphoria. This classic chart below shows exactly what we are feeling when the markets are doing their thing. What we need to do is stop feeling and start automating and put a system in place. Maybe just put money away and save the stress for your advisor. That's what they get paid to do anyways: worry for you. You don't need to. Remember when the bottom of the stock market falls out, chances are there are way, *way* bigger problems in the world anyways, so there's not much you can do, and remember almost everyone you know is in the same boat—whether they admit to it or not. We are always emotional around money.

Key point 8: Try to take the emotion out when investing, but don't take the emotion out of the dreams you are working to fund. It's important to note that emotions usually get in the way of a good financial plan.

THE CYCLE OF MARKET EMOTIONS CHART

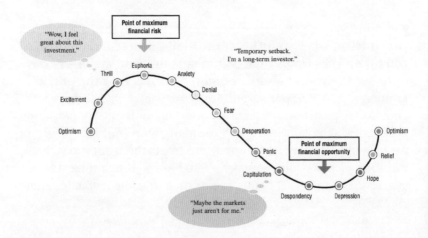

This is the emotional psychology behind investing, or the feelings an investor feels as he goes through the investment cycle.

The point of maximum financial opportunity is ideally where you should buy, although typically when we should be buying, our emotions are running the ship and they steer us the wrong way because we are feeling fear, desperation, and panic, and in no way will emotion let logic take over and run the ship. Emotion at this point is like Lisa and her Cadbury Fruit & Nut chocolate bar—you dare not get in between us if you want to live!

The point of maximum financial risk is when everything seems to be going fantastic and everyone agrees with you. That is when you should sell, although at that point the champagne is flowing and the party is in full swing, so why sell your position and bring that great "feeling" to a complete stop?

As humans, the FOMO (fear of missing out) drives us to do crazy things, sometimes in relation to investing. This typically happens when we are close to the top of a market or sitting at or around "*thrill,*" especially when everyone is having a party and telling you to jump on the bandwagon and buy that bio-tech company that will be like winning the lottery. I relate FOMO to sneaking out with my roommate in college past curfew to meet up at a pub with some cute guys from our dorm. Sleep is overrated, anyways.

FOMO has always been my thing; it actually pushes us forward to try new things. So it's not always a bad thing. It's just something to be aware of, and when it comes to investing, maybe try to take emotion and fear out of the equation and let logic prevail. I know this is *much* easier said than done, especially when in college and even more so when everyone around you will be a millionaire before you if you don't invest in that hot stock or real estate right now.

Then we swing to the other side of market emotions where FOF (fear of failure) is presumed. This is where we have "failed" in our heads and feel the need to sell and get out, cut our losses, and move forward. This isn't always the best approach. Don't get me wrong: there are many times in life when we need to cut our losses and move forward. This is when I caution you to let logic prevail and add in your sixth sense (women have powerful sixth senses!). Trust your gut.

Also, **key point 9: Get a financial plan or Investment Policy Statement (IPS) as this will also help make sure you have a plan in place.** As advisors, we create these for you, so when you are "freaking out" we can remind you of the plan we put in place to help weather the storm.

Don't forget: storms are needed in life. Storms are what make us appreciate the good times. If you never feel the bottom, then you will never know the highs, so these cycles are good things. Be thankful for your trials, because let me be the first to tell you a whole lotta rainbows are coming your way soon – trials and down markets spell o-p-p-o-r-t-u-n-i-t-y!

Also, did I mention cash flow is king? Companies that produce solid dividends are usually a good idea. Dividend funds, or individual companies that offer dividends, are worth looking into!

Key point 10: When the fear of missing out, fear of failure, fear that the economy will collapse, or fear of any kind rears its ugly head, then it's time to reframe your brain, add logic, and strip away crazy emotion. This will probably help lead to better financial decisions, rid you of some of the fear, and allow you to take the appropriate financial action.

Key point 11: The market is not the economy, and the economy is not the market. Although most people will assume both are perfectly correlated, they aren't. At times, they may fluctuate in sync and they aren't fully mutually exclusive, but people often confuse that they are one and the same.

Not to mention, which economy or market are we talking about, anyways? There are sixty-four regulated markets in the world as well as all the markets that aren't listed and thousands of economies.

A variety of things can affect a market, such as someone dumping a load of money into it, which would drive prices higher (supply and demand). It's the same as the government throwing billions of dollars into the economy to stimulate job creation or offering tax incentives. Monetary policy, which is macroeconomic plans put into place by central banks, will also drive markets as central banks influence money supply. The same goes for fiscal policy, which is when the plans are put into place to adjust government spending, and tax policies with the aim to control the economic conditions by various governments and regulatory bodies.

While I won't go deep into this topic right now, just know that even though my specific Alberta economy is not too hot as I write this, some economies in the world are doing better, and some stock markets are doing crappy. Meanwhile, other markets are humming along okay. Opportunities are everywhere.

Key point 12: Don't forget: money flows to where it's cheapest! People always want a deal. People also want to save money. If you need a loan, you will hunt out the best rates. That's what we do. (Now, that's not saying that the terms and conditions of that money are the best, such as the subprime teaser rates circa 2008!) My office lease was up, and instead of renewing at the current rates, I shopped around for new space, thus saving $600 a month. It was a no-brainer. Money wants to be efficient, and it will always flow to where you think you are getting a "deal."

Key point 13: Money is constantly in motion. If you think when you deposit your money at the bank that it sits in a vault till you need it again, you are sadly mistaken. My generation knows that; however, I believe my Oma's generation did not. Money is *always* in flow. It is being lent out (and I'm not even going to touch on fractional banking in this book!), and it is in motion. When it is not in motion, sadly, it's actually not doing anyone any favours. Money works best when it's put to work. When it's sitting stagnant, it isn't providing value. We need money to form capital to provide the seed money for new projects and businesses. Money being in motion is what propels humanity forward. For every new idea, new drug, new cure, new tech, and new fuel source, money flows to fund these ideas, sometimes privately and sometimes from the capital or public markets. If people didn't invest and hid their money under their mattress, then money would stop flowing into these ventures at some point, and we would stop progressing, unless the government stepped in and did what it wanted. Okay, that's kinda dramatic, but I think you see my point here, anyways. Also, if we weren't actively growing our money or wealth, then the government would have less tax revenue from us, and then that opens up a whole other shoebox—but we'll save that for a Facebook rant.

Key point 14: Hire a great financial coach (they will help you hire a great money manager in return!). We already beat this do death with our flip-flops chapter, but it's so important that it deserves another flog (see "Pair 2"). You hire pros to do this work; that's their passion. I'm guessing you aren't a financial professional geek who lives on Bay or Wall Street and knows the ins and outs of the investment world. Great! 'Cause I didn't write this book for the 1,000 people who work on Bay Street; it's written for the millions of us that don't eat, breathe, and live this stuff.

Your financial coach will make sure you are well diversified, hold your hand, force you at times to make the right decision when all you want to do is give up, and be there to encourage you to keep going. They will make sure you have stocks, bonds, REITs (Real Estate Investment Trusts), and multinational companies, ETFs, etc., in your portfolio, or make sure you have the right mix and are well diversified.

Your financial coach needs to be a great overseer of the money manager, making sure he's doing what he was hired to do. You and your advisor may have to fire or hire new money managers from time to time when circumstantial changes happen, or when unsystematic risk (risk that can be reduced through diversification) is not dealt with. When systematic risk occurs (this is the risk that you can't diversify your way out of, the unpredictable events that effect everything, such as a huge earthquake or war or terrorism), then it's not time for a manager change. It's just bad luck for everyone left holding the bag at that point.

Key point 15: Financial and investment advisors don't work for free. Even if you aren't directly cutting a cheque to your advisor at the bank or your independent advisor, he is still getting paid. Everything relating to money has a fee as does every transaction. So here's the thing: if you are not paying directly out of your pocket, you are better off finding an advisor who will answer your phone calls, return your emails, and work with you in future years rather than one whose name you don't even know or recall. Obviously, if you are cutting a cheque and paying a fee for advice, you will make sure you hire someone awesome. At the end of the day, like any relationships, communication goes both ways. An advisor can help you out only with what you ask for help with. Duh! But clearly asking for help is something our pride gets in the way of! So......

Key point 16: Ask lots of questions, and ask for help!

Key point 17: Dollar-cost average (DCA) your way into quality investments. Dollar-cost averaging is when you buy a little every month or as often as you can. Why is DCA brilliant? Because you can still make money (for the most part) in a sideways or flat or volatile market. I don't want to start a hot debate (okay, maybe I do) over this subject, however, you can decide for yourself. Reviewing years of research on this subject, if you had dollar-cost averaged into a quality investment fund or stock, you minimize your long-term risk. This isn't a cure-all, and it doesn't protect against a falling market. At the end of the day, I believe DCA allows for most people to sleep better at night. If you are for or against this, either way, it brings me to my next point.

People always ask me if there is a good time to buy and get in the market. The best time was yesterday; there is no good time. This next statement is probably much older than me.

Key point 18: It's not timing the markets; it's time in the markets. (And yes, I know I've mentioned this before in Pair 2, but it bears repeating.) It's like waiting for a good time to have kids! Hahaha—anyone who has kids *know*s there is *no* good time to have kids! You just go for it, and go for it with gusto ... jump in with both feet, and don't look back!

Now, it's time for a closer look at the main risks you need to be aware of in relationship to your portfolio. Here is a list of risks your money faces when you invest:

⌐ Inflation risk: the goal is to outpace inflations. (Hint: At the time of writing this, GICs in Canada do not outpace inflation right now, meaning you are technically getting a negative return on your money.)

⌐ Currency risk: be aware when you are buying a stock in another currency, even if the stock goes up, you can still lose money if the currency is devaluing against yours.

⌐ Interest rate risk: the goal is to reduce the risk of changing interest rates, in either direction, which can affect the value of your investment, depending on what you are investing in.

⌐ Volatility risk: this is the risk of your investments fluctuating dramatically.

⌐ Liquidity risk: this is how easily you can sell your investment, or you are locked in for a long time, or it takes a while to find a buyer for your investment.

⌐ Political risk: this includes the government's control over a change in legislation that impacts your investment.

I'm sure we could list these all day, which brings me to...

Key point 19: Know the risks involved, and know your risk tolerance. This also goes back to key point 16: ask lots of questions! One way to protect against inflation is to hold stocks of publically traded companies (equities). As an economy grows and expands, inflation increases, which means the costs of goods go up in price, which typically means the value of the business also increases (note that I didn't necessarily say "profits," although that can happen, too). When you hold and own quality stocks in your portfolio, this will help protect your purchasing power over the long term.

Besides having a great financial coach, understanding the only constant is change, diversifying your portfolio, dollar-cost averaging, understanding the main risks to your portfolio, and making sure to disclose your full financial picture to your coach, is there anything else you need to know? *No*; the answer for today's lesson on investment 101 is no. Everything else is probably noise, a deterrent. You can build a solid financial plan on these principles. If you listen to your coach, dollar-cost average into your investments where possible, stay diversified, and create a plan and stick with it through annual reviews (note: I'm not saying just talk once a year—obviously life happens when life happens, so plan for and commit to a yearly review and goals with your coach), then providence will move with you. You have to believe in your plan as well. I really believe this, and I have seen it time and time again with my clients.

Okay, there is actually a lot more to say about this topic and millions of books to read; however, for the purposes of this conversation, I'm going to say this is what you need to know to get started. You will learn everything else over time, and even if you dislike this topic, this chapter should be enough knowledge to at least point you in the right direction.

Here's what's worse: remember when we talked about what the real risks are in investing? The biggest risk is *not doing anything*. Life will move on with or without you. Not doing anything is like sitting in the middle of a sample sale or Boxing Day sale and looking at your perfect pair of shoes, in your size, at 50 percent off, and not being sure if they are going to drop lower in price, so you wait. Meanwhile, the pushy redhead next to you grabs them and gets the deal of her life. You waited, you let the opportunity pass you by, and ultimately, you are sitting there paralyzed in the middle of Nordstrom's left behind, all alone, without your new fave shoes. End Scene. (I just shed a tear—please don't let this be you!)

You gotta try, as doing nothing will get you nothing. As my partner has said, you have to play the lottery to win. I hate it when he's right. Although I think it's a complete waste of money to play the lottery (I prefer putting $20 on blackjack, at least having fun while losing my money), but you will never win if you never play.

Now, let's shift gears into some simple strategies for perhaps something many Canadians are currently doing anyways: RRSPs. Oh, and let me be the first to tell you, I don't believe RRSPs are the best tax route for everyone! They are, however, a great tax tool when need be.

Key point 20: You will need to consult your coaching team (accountant or advisor) on what type of account is best for you for tax purposes when it comes to saving and investing your

money, and you will need to discuss the tax consequences of your different options. If you do plan on placing money in an RRSP account, I'm going to show you how to get 20 to 66.66 percent more into your RRSP every year without saving any more money!

Keeping in step with this book (ha—puns crack me up!), I'm going to compare these strategies to shoes. If you think like me, you will know flats are okay, kitten heels are a bit higher and mightier, but a night out on the town warrants killer sexy stilettos where your legs look fabulous and elongated (or that's what I tell myself), even if you can wear them for only five minutes. I also created a little chart at the end of this section to demonstrate the power of these three strategies.

Here they are:

The Flat Shoe:

Put money into your RRSP. Period. Most Canadians don't.

According to Stats Canada, 23.4 percent of tax filers in 2013 contributed to an RRSP. And fair enough: if you aren't making much in the way of income, I wouldn't recommend it, and I would use an alternative shoe for saving; however, most Canadians don't even save on a regular basis in any account, RRSP or not!

So here's the point: *Save.* Save monthly if you can—dollar-cost averaging is always best!

If you are in the top marginal tax bracket, it is one of the few tax deductions available to you if you are an employee, so just do it. Put on the *flat* shoe and do it. Otherwise, you are basically barefoot.

Important: Don't miss this paragraph! Here are the numbers. I'm going to use an example of a client saving $10,000 a year for all my examples. If you put in $10,000 to your RRSP and you are in the top marginal tax bracket (approximately 40 percent), you will get a refund of approximately $4,000 in Alberta (this varies province-to-province, and by how much income you actually make). Any accountant can help you calculate this amount for your personal tax situation, or your financial planner can do that as well. The money in your RRSP grows tax deferred until you pull it out, and then it is taxed fully as your income at that time.

The Kitten Heel:

Wanna spice up your savings and go out on the town in a comfortable kitten heel? This is an easy boost in your RRSP savings, still saving only $10,000 a year.

Figure out how much you are getting back as a tax return. In the example above, you were getting back $4,000.

Because you know you are getting that $4,000 as a tax refund, why not invest it when you get it? If you do reinvest your return money and continue to do that over the years, you will now invest $14,000 every year instead of the $10,000 you are saving up. It will boost your savings by about 40 percent—that's *huge* over the years. See the chart below.

Or if you really need new shoes for that new trip, why not reinvest at least half of it, and blow the rest like you normally do? You will still get a 20 percent boost on your savings. I know my girls need a little quality shopping time, too!

The Stiletto:

Ready to rock and make your portfolio extra hot? This is the ultimate RRSP strategy to boost your savings and make your portfolio sizzle!

Same $10,000 saved. Same example, but this time, we know already that we are going to put in $10,000 and get refunded $4,000.

So what do you do? You get an RRSP loan for $6,666.66 during that current tax year. (Yes, I know—I picked bad example numbers! *Yikes!*)

You invested $10,000 plus the $6,666.66 loan for a total of $16,666.66 into your RRSP. Your tax refund is $6,666.66, which you use to pay off the RRSP loan you took out.

Here's the fancy-schmancy math formula that provides the loan amount needed to equal the tax refund:

$$\frac{(\text{cash on hand} \times \text{marginal tax rate})}{(100\% - \text{marginal tax rate})} = \text{LOAN AMOUNT}$$

$$\frac{(\$10,000 \times 40\%)}{(60\%)} = \$6,666.66$$

Here's an example: let's say it's December 2015. You have your $10,000 RRSP money saved in your bank account (or, if you are smart, you've been investing a little every month, dollar-cost averaging!). Either way, you call me up—yes, me, your trusted financial advisor—and I hook you up with an RRSP loan from one of *many* financial institutions (RRSP loans are easy to get, very inexpensive, and very short term—typically two to three months in duration, from the time you take it out until you file your return, get your refund, and pay it back). Then you take out an RRSP loan for $6,666.66. Then you file your taxes.

You receive a tax refund in the amount of $6,666.66 because you put into your RRSP $16,666.66 ($10,000 you had plus loan of $6,666.66).

That's a boost of 66.66 percent into your retirement savings! Check out the chart below to see how your retirement savings look over time.

The loan for a couple of months may cost you $40 to $100 (about $22 a month) at 4 percent; interest-only payments on a loan of $6,666.66. That's small potatoes!

I'm not sure why most people don't do this. Oh yeah … *because my industry does a bad job of sharing this powerful strategy!*

But guess what! In all three scenarios, you still saved $10,000. No more, no less. This strategy is huge, ladies! (Be a smarty-pants and show this to your husband or show off at the next office cocktail party.)

This strategy also works with any amount you have saved for your RRSP. I know I can do RRSP loans as small as $1,000—so there are no excuses for you not to boost your RRSP savings by doing either "heeled" strategy, kitten or stiletto!

When you *do* any of these strategies or want help with your RRSP planning, please *call me*! I don't just value financial planning; I also value a good shopping spree and wine. Who said you can't have it all? *The truth is,* you can have it all—with some smart planning!

Wanna see the final numbers? (I'm assuming you invest this money once annually with 6 percent annual compound growth at the end of the year for a client saving $10,000 every year, utilizing the three strategies with a marginal tax bracket of 40 percent.)

	FLAT	**KITTEN**	**STILETTO**
Year 1	$10,000	$14,000	$16,667
Year 2	$20,600	$28,840	$34,334
Year 5	$56,371	$78,919	$93,953
Year 10	$131,808	$184,531	$219,684
Year 20	$367,856	$514,998	$613,105
Year 25	**$548,645**	**$768,103**	**$914,427**

The small print: The information contained herein is based on certain assumptions and is for illustration purposes only. While care is taken in the preparation of this chart, no warranty is made as to the accuracy or applicability in any particular case. Please speak to your accountant and/or financial advisor regarding your own tax situation or before you implement any of these strategies. You need to have sufficient contribution room available to utilize these strategies.

Lisa Elle

FUN SHOE FACT: Socrates once claimed, "When our feet hurt, we hurt all over."

SOLE QUOTE: "You are either in your bed or in your shoes; it pays to invest in both." —John Wildsmith

SOUL QUOTE: "If you can count your money, you don't have a billion dollars." —J. Paul Getty

FAB READS:

- *Money: Master the Game* by Tony Robbins
- *Simple Wealth, Inevitable Wealth* by Nick Murray
- *Practically Investing: Smart Investment Techniques Your Neighbour Doesn't Know About* by Coreen T. Sol
- *The Intelligent Investor: The Definitive Book on Value Investing* by Benjamin Graham

SHOUT IT OUT: I am a good steward over the money and resources placed in my care.

PUTTIN' ON THE SHOES:

- Start saving something!
- Create a plan to invest, or hire someone to create one for you.

SHOEBOX NOTES:

- When it comes to investing, it's okay to get average returns—remember that always makes you above average in many more ways!

Strut

➘ It's not about shooting for the stars with your returns, but if you're slow and steady, you will make the moon.

STRUT TUNES:

➘ "Happy" by Pharrell Williams

➘ "I'm Coming Out" by Diana Ross

➘ "Roar" by Katy Perry

➘ "Life is a Highway" by Tom Cochrane

11

Flats

Smart women have at least one pair of flat shoes. Remember: diversification is key for a spicy life and shoe closet.

STYLE DESCRIPTION: A women's show with a flat heel or no heel, typically a slip-on shoe.

PROSPERITY DESCRIPTION: Real estate, such as flats, is part of a great diversified portfolio.

I **swear the** goddess of creativity just handed me this book on a silver platter sometimes! This chapter is about real estate.

I always wanted to have an apartment and call it my "flat" like the Brits do; it's another dream of the Canadian girl and the result of too many British rom-coms.

I'm in Montreal right now, and I've plunked myself down at the Ritz-Carlton because I like nice real estate, and fancy hotels are just that—some great real estate. Yup, I just show up and sit in lobbies of nice hotels and write, usually till concierge boots me out. But today, I've made a few concierge friends ... Bonjour, Markus! It's rather inspiring, actually—especially the people watching.

I'm not a real estate expert at all; however, I've had my share of real estate dealings, and I am surrounded by amazing real estate experts, so most of what I am going to tell you is from what I have learned from them. Plus, I *did* sell well over $50 million of real estate for a new homebuilder in a past life—so I may know a little more than I let on! Oh, and if I'm being totally truthful here, I've made really bad real estate purchases (as well as some good ones). When I was twenty-eight, my partner and I had five rental properties, and I rented out *my* first place when I was twenty-three. I've had some luck, but I *will* say I've spent way more than I've made on some of these properties, so it's not all positive news! Some people think real estate is a "safer" investment than investing in quality stocks, and you already know what I'm going to say. *Nothing* is safe. And nothing is better, and nothing is worse. You need to be well diversified. Period.

So I'll share the knowledge I've learned over the years with you as it pertains to real estate. Let's start with the basics. We all have probably learned that we should own property and pay down something versus let money go to rent to pay off someone else's mortgage. I want to say to my ladies who do rent, that is not bad. I have rented in the past, and I still rent my office. It's so nice to know you are not on the hook when something breaks down or repairs need to be made. So I will never say to someone that owning or renting is better – it is what is best for *your* situation: your job, your lifestyle, and what works for you!

Key point 1: Houses cost money: upkeep, renovations, roofs, etc. So if you rent, just remember that you don't have to worry about it when the water heater breaks or you need a new roof. If you own, you have to save that money yourself. I have just forked out over $5,000 in repairs on one of my properties in the last six months for unexpected repairs, appliances crapping out, and so forth. And this stuff needs to be paid pronto – so you don't get a choice; you need to come up with the money, and quite frankly, it does suck. Let's face it – you aren't going to live without hot water if your water tank craps out.

Key point 2: If you do want to buy a rental property, the rental market is alive and well, and it isn't going away. Regardless of what side of the coin you are on—owning or renting—renters will always have their place in this world. People are always moving due to job relocation, and relationships (unfortunately) are always ending, and kids are always moving out, causing a permanent long-term need for rental properties. Plus, when it comes to commercial space, you are lucky if you own and don't lease.

When we have a constant in life, we can make informed decisions based on that information. Similar to the way we can do tax planning or buy life insurance for things we know are going to happen down the road, rental properties will always be in demand; while the market will fluctuate from time to time, in general, people always need a place to live in good and bad times.

Knowing that constant, whether you rent or own your own home, and if you can afford to, it's a good idea to have a rental property if you can swing it. The benefit is that someone else will be paying down your mortgage, building equity for you. And if you wait twenty-five years, chances are that as all real estate and markets trend up over the long term, you will probably get some capital appreciation, too. So even if you do what I did and buy at the peak, you know at the end of the day, if the properties are paying for themselves, it will work out okay. And really, if it doesn't, well, life happens. You have to try to be okay with that. There is no such thing as a guarantee in life.

So why do people still expect guarantees with their real estate and investments? Beats me; be okay with letting it go! Most times, investing in something you've researched and made a sound financial decision around usually works in your favour. But if it doesn't, that's okay. You have to keep moving forward. It's all part of the game.

Key point 3: Make sure common sense prevails (not just emotion):

- If you do buy real estate, remember for resale that the less expensive it is, the more buyers there will be for it. For example, your $7 million house may not sell as fast as your $200,000 condo because more people can afford a $200,000 house versus a $7 million house, so your market will be bigger in general.

- Buy near public transportation or with a good walking distance to a store.

- If you are buying vacation property, remember that it's a vacation property. In a bad market, nobody wants a vacation property; meanwhile, people in large cities still need a place to live, so a smaller, affordable place will always rent or sell faster than a place out in Bora Bora or the boonies, even if the latter is on the lake with a convenience store ten miles away.

- If you can find a fabulous rental management company to handle your property for a good price, go for it. It's one less headache you need to deal with. It kind of turns your property portfolio into your own mini REIT (Real Estate Investment Trust), and it leaves you feeling less like a mean-ol'-landlord, because you can take a hands-off approach.

- Be careful with leveraging. Leveraging—or, in this case, pulling out equity from your property to purchase another one or make another investment—can be very risky, just keep that in mind; if the new investment does not pan out, you need to be okay with that and be able to sleep okay at night. (Really, sleep is important, people! Never do anything to jeopardize that ... although I did have children ... hmmm.)

- Yes, if you need your mortgage insured through CMHC (Canada Mortgage and Housing Corporation), or Genworth Canada, or whomever to insure your high-ratio mortgage to get you into the market and into your own home, do it. Usually, over time, good or bad, you'll most likely be glad you did it. Money aside, there is a huge sense of pride when you own your own home, and it's important to take pride in your home. There are worse things you can spend your money on (and trust me, as people of instant gratification, we do!) The lending rules in Canada are pretty solid anyways, and it's not easy to get a mortgage at the time I write this. They are pretty strict since the 2008 financial melt-down, and they do not want that to happen in Canada, so they make sure you have a good job, good credit, and so forth.

↳ Common sense says to pay down debt. But again, balance the tax-deductible debt. Pay off the non-tax-deductible debt first! For example, your husband dies and leaves you money. You pay off your principal residence first! That is non-tax-deductible debt in Canada (different story in the US). Don't pay off your rental property first. You are still using the interest as a tax deduction.

↳ Building equity is building equity; yes, it may be notional at times, which means it's just all fake until you crystallize your gains or losses and also implies that until the day you actually sell and have the money in your hand, all losses or gains are virtually fictitious. With that said, obviously your home is building equity as you pay it down. So, yes, do include that on your net worth or when you are having a bad month and "feel" like you are saving nothing (yes, I've had many, many of those months!). Just remember: you are building on one side of the balance sheet of "You Financial Inc."

Let's look at a rental property purchase from an investment stand and cash flow stand. First of all, in general terms, an economic cycle is typically four to seven years by some economist standards (some say two to ten years but always cyclical nonetheless). Keep this in mind.

Here's an example: if you bought a property for $200,000 outright (no mortgage) and over time it appreciates to $250,000, you have a capital gain of $50,000.

Meanwhile, over the years, you rented it out for, say, $1,300 per month, minus property taxes, condo fees, and whatever utilities you agreed to pay on behalf of your renter. Let's say you clear $1,000 a month after those expenses. This becomes a $12,000 income stream off your original $200,000 investment—a 6 percent rate of return on your money. Not bad. However, you do have to factor in assessments if you own a condo—such as damage, unrented months, housing repairs, appliance repairs, and so on—so that dips into your cash flow (this I know from experience all too well.)

Now, if you net after all that even 5 percent, plus the capital gain you receive when you sell the property (assuming your property has gone up in value—this again is a big assumption!), then you will be netting more over all. If you held the property for five years and it grew from $200,000 to $250,000, then your overall net gain in this example would have been 8 percent from the cash flow every year, plus the $50,000. (And right now we aren't talking tax consequences, but all in all, $12,000 multiplied by the five years you had it rented out plus the $50,000 equals $110,000, or a 55 percent return on your money over five years, then divide back over the five years to equal 11 percent per year return on your money.)

There are probably easier ways to make 11 percent return on your money. And just like investing in a quality mutual fund or stock, there is no guarantee here, either—for some reason, most people think that real estate is "safer" than investing in quality companies. Remember, one or two unrented months plus repairs and your net cash flow and return have probably just reduced dramatically.

I don't think you can go wrong by diversifying—so why not do both? But point in fact, a mutual fund will never call you up in the middle of the night and say it needs a new water heater.

I have had clients over the years who would buy rental properties only if they could net over 10 percent per year, based on what they thought the market would do or from what rent they thought they could get. Owning a rental property is adding value—you are providing a home for someone who, for whatever reason or circumstance, cannot purchase on his own and needs a place to live.

I also think that if you have a mortgage on your rental properties (as I do), it's okay. I think that if you are going to hold a property (even if you aren't making any cash flow monthly or yearly) that, looking at the big picture, in twenty-five years or less, you will have an asset that is paid off, which you can sell or continue renting to draw retirement income.

Key point 4: People keep saying they aren't making land anymore. This is true; however, there's still a lot of land to go around. So don't always get caught in the hype. I've seen many land deals or potential land developers go bankrupt—actually, I've seen *too* many. Typically, these are private equity deals. You just need to be aware of the supply and demand and really understand the area where you want invest.

Have you heard of Tianducheng? There, you will find a replica of Paris in China—which is a total ghost town! (I'm sure you've heard of this; if not, Google it! It's fascinating!) China had its own bubble and now has twelve-lane, brand-new highways that are totally deserted. I bring the up to illustrate my point on supply and demand. Just keep that always in the back of your head when you think of anything financial. You could have the best idea or product in the world, but if no one wants it, then it's worthless. We create value. We decide what's important or not, what's valuable or not. I think China's Paris looks super cool; maybe I'll be able to go one day. However, it probably won't fill up for twenty years. Who wants to sit around on a dud of an investment and wait twenty years for it to "pick up"? Just my two cents.

FUN SHOE FACT: Women are four times more likely to have foot problems than men are, mostly due to footwear. This probably does not shock you; vanity has a price.

SOLE QUOTE: "All the Wicked Witch ever wanted was a good pair of shoes." —Unknown

"If you don't think shoes are important, just ask Dorothy and Cinderella." —Unknown

SOUL QUOTE: "Financial freedom is when you never do anything that you don't want to do for money and you never omit doing something that you want to do because of lack of money." —Phil Laut

Strut

"Be who you are and say what you feel, because those who mind don't matter, and those who matter don't mind." —Dr. Seuss

FAB READS:

⌐ *97 Tips for Canadian Real Estate Investors* by Don R. Campbell, Barry McGuire, and Russell Westcott

⌐ *Thinking, Fast and Slow* by Daniel Kahneman

SHOUT IT OUT: Resources and money flow easily to me.

PUTTIN' ON THE SHOES:

⌐ If you are considering purchasing a rental property or already own one – go to www.ellementsgroup.com/realestateplanner to calculate your estimated return and see whether it is a good investment for you – according to your standards.

⌐ Also at www.ellementsgroup.com/realestateplanner, you will get "10 Tips Before you buy Real Estate."

SHOEBOX NOTES:

⌐ Real estate is a great diversification, such as owning a home or purchasing a rental property.

⌐ Calculate your return on investment (ROI) by carefully weighing the return and the potential pitfalls or headaches.

STRUT TUNES:

⌐ "Empire State of Mind" by Jay Z and Alicia Keys

⌐ "Dreams" by The Cranberries

⌐ "Cheek to Cheek" by Lady Gaga and Tony Bennett

12
Wedges

"The woman who walks alone is likely to find herself in places no one has ever been before." —Albert Einstein

STYLE DESCRIPTION: A women's shoe formed by a roughly triangular or wedge like piece that extends from the front or middle to the back.

PROSPERITY DESCRIPTION: At some point, you will find yourself single, separated, divorced, or widowed, and you will no longer have a partner, for better or worse—so you better get your financial house organized before it gets worse.

I have a rather large excel spreadsheet, when printed off, is eight pages that I need to tape together—that's how big it is. The document is called "If Lisa Dies" (yes, how disturbing!), and it outlines every account, from my utilities account numbers, passport numbers, and healthcare accounts, and also details where the wills and safety deposit box keys are located. It's a detailed description of what's what; it's a means of taking stock of everything we are stewards of. So when one of us dies, or we get divorced, or the person who normally takes care of the bills is mentally or physically incapable to manage the family finances, then this go-to page becomes the Holy Grail. These unpleasant situations *will* arise, because let's face it: divorce, separation, health issues, and/or death are going to affect us all—some beautiful women bear the lifetime struggle of all four. I know a lot of amazing women on their second or third marriage, and if there is one thing I know it's that no one is immune to these things, be it cancer or divorce.

So we need to be organized and take steps to make sure that *when* these things happen, it's not going to devastate us or our families financially.

Here are my three things all women need to have, married or not:

🠔 A credit card in their own name—one that's not joint with their partner.

🠔 A "stash of cash" hidden in their house or close surroundings. (I recommend enough to cover two months' rent or hotel rooms and enough to live off of for a month; so for me, that might be $3,000 to $10,000, enough to live on but not enough to be devastated if it was ever stolen, lost, or destroyed in a fire/waterproof safe.) This is money your partner does not need to know about. It's not a secret; it's you protecting your family—Mama Bear kind of stuff! Hey, if your partner doesn't pay attention to this kind of detail, then you need to take the bull by the horns and step up and take care of your family. So turn that feeling of guilt around, and don't feel bad for making provisions for your family (plus, if you have a partner who would spend that money, then you don't tell him about it!), in case you one day find yourself in an undesirable situation, and another example would be fire, or if you were forced out of your home for any number of reasons.

↳ A chequing account in your own name, preferably at a bank where you do not do all your banking currently. You are allowed to open an account anywhere, and some are free, so this won't even cost you anything. Keep a little money in there.

I can give you a million reasons why you need these three things, but I won't. You can let your brain go wild. However, whether it is death or divorce, you may find yourself in a position one day and you will be glad you did this and that you knew enough to protect yourself from whatever personal or financial situation you may find yourself in—or whatever "wedges" its way into your life!

What you need to do it this: *build a reserve*! The army has reserves, so why shouldn't you? A reserve is the extra, the more than you need, the auxiliary options for life. The reserve is the giver of choices for your life.

I don't envy any woman who has to endure a separation or divorce of any kind. I also don't envy women who have lost their partners or loved ones. And the truth of the matter is that unless you end up like Ali and Noah in *The Notebook* (spoiler alert) and you die in the arms of your true love at the same time, then you will experience the end of a relationship in your lifetime. Whether it's good, bad, or ugly ... none of it's fun. There is no easy fix for this inevitable event; however, there are ways to stay on the ball, even if you still prefer your partner handle all the financial matters in your home. Sometimes you just need to ask a few simple questions to make sure that things are on track, and in reality, you just need to do some of the heavy lifting in regards to planning once and then tweak it every year or quarter in your spreadsheet or whatever tracking and planning tool you use.

Truth be told, I'm partial to my romantic comedies, although every now and then I've always liked a little gunfight, the odd car chase, or even *The Terminator*. He *did* always threaten he'd be back ... (this week, in a movie theater near you).

Well, here's the thing (another spoiler alert!), unlike *The Terminator*, in real life, when we die, we are dead. We are *not* coming back (*gasp!*), yet it keeps taking thousands of people by surprise every year. *Crazy, right?!*

Strut

What's even more shocking is how many Canadians die without a will or die intestate.

According to a 2012 survey by LAWPRO, 56 percent of Canadians do not have a will. This I know to be true because I ask all my clients whether they have one, and it is at the base of all my financial planning efforts. Plus, you have no idea what a huge gift a will is to your family who is stressed and left sorting out the remainder of your estate, wanting to fulfill and respect your wishes.

A will is the foundation of a good financial plan. It not only lets you direct how your assets are distributed, but it also forces self-reflection, as well as one of my favourite planning principles that Stephen Covey made famous, "begin with the end in mind."[23] Knowing what we are building, getting clear, and painting that picture also helps propel us towards our goals. There are intestacy provisions, which vary from province to province. However, they probably won't reflect the true wishes of most individuals, especially if you fall into any of these categories:

- If you wish your spouse to receive your entire estate

- If you're in your second marriage

- If you're in a common-law relationship

- If you're in a in same-sex relationship

- If you have children from a previous marriage or born outside of marriage

- If you have a child with special circumstances

- If you do not want a public trustee or government managing assets for your minor children

- If you don't want your kids to get their hands on all that money at age eighteen or nineteen

- If you wish to do any tax planning whatsoever

- If you wish to leave any money to charity

23 Stephen Covey, *The Seven Habits of Highly Successful People: Restoring the Character Ethic* (New York: Simon and Schuster, 1989).

⌐ If you wish to appoint guardians for your minor children (and you definitely don't want crazy Auntie B doing that!)

⌐ If you wish to grant extended powers to your executor

⌐ If you wish to establish trusts for your loved ones (so Johnny Jr. doesn't get a $100,000 sports car at age eighteen)

⌐ If you wish to leave money to your favourite financial coach … (PM me for my banking details)

And finally, you need to have a will because who doesn't want to have the last word—it's something most of us are good at anyways!

And one last little wedge that rears its ugly head from time to time: money schemes. I've had many clients and close friends lose thousands on a Ponzi scheme or other such financial scheme where it's taken them years to recover, long after the men responsible have been released from jail. My advice is this—trust your gut! If it seems too good to be true, it usually is. Here's the thing: always look for the value add and intention. If it's just to get rich, personally I don't think that's a good enough reason. If you believe in the cause and want to throw a little money in something—go for it! It's risk-reward. Remember that a good rule of thumb is to not put more than 5 to 10 percent of your net worth in something so risky. This isn't just for Ponzi schemes or pyramid schemes; it also goes for a high-risk stocks and private equity investments, start-up businesses, etc. I've mentioned this before; being able to sleep at night is more valuable than putting all your chips down on black.

When all else fails, run this quick investment check in your HEAD:

H: Helping create value. What value will investing in this company/opportunity bring, and/or how is it helping others/ society/advancing humanity? What is the end product or game plan?

E: Earnings—Rate of Return on Investment. Is it too good to be true, or do the numbers seem to make sense?

A: Accounting. Check on these things: tax consequences/tax planning, diminishing returns, and legalities/legitimacy. Did you get a prospectus/formal information/financial statements on the investment? And even more importantly, *did you read it?*

D: Dreams. How is this helping fund your dreams? Why are you investing in this? Will it bring you closer to your dreams or pull you away from them? Will seeing this money disappear result in a loss of lifestyle?

And above all, while doing HEAD checks, don't forget to check your *gut!* Women have an amazing sixth sense—trust your instincts, and don't buy to please anyone else. I know that FOMO (fear of missing out) of "the investment of a life time" is sometimes greater than the fear of loss. We want to belong and be part of the "club," and therefore we feel we *need* to do these investments or start-up businesses when "everyone else" is doing it at the expense of our own dreams or goals or even common sense.

FUN SHOE FACT: The most common injury incurred from wearing high heels is a sprained ankle (I know that's so shocking!), and did you know that heel pain and ingrown toenails are the most common problems researched online?

SOLE QUOTE: "If I ever let my head down, it will only be to admire my shoes." —Marilyn Monroe

SOUL QUOTE: "One of the hardest parts of life is choosing whether to walk away or try harder." —Ziad K. Abdelnour

Lisa Elle

"Who you *were*, who you *are*, and who you'll *be* are three different people! Don't let the person you *were* have any say in the person you will *be*." —Lisa's twist on a Robert Tew quote

FAB READS:

- *The Secret* by Rhonda Byrne

- *Thrive: The Third Metric to Redefining Success and Creating a Life of Well-Being, Wisdom, and Wonder* by Arianna Huffington

- *Rework* by Jason Fried and David Heinemeier Hansson

SHOUT IT OUT: My abundance is constantly increasing.

PUTTIN' ON THE SHOES:

- Keep three things for yourself: a bank account, a credit card, and a stash of cash.

- Always ask questions! Always! Ignorance will only hurt you financially.

- Use my online Kick-Asset Tracker at www.ellementsgroup.com/tracker

SHOEBOX NOTES:

- Be aware. Ask questions.

- Know what you own, what is in your name, what you have, what you signed for.

- Keep track, always! You—not someone else!

STRUT TUNES:

- "These Boots Are Made For Walkin'" by Nancy Sinatra

- "Shake It Off" by Taylor Swift

- "Chicken Fried" by Zac Brown Band

13

Stilettos

Heels are good—they leave a mark on the world!
Finding your financial strength will help you strut.

STYLE DESCRIPTION: A women's shoe with a very high, thin heel.

PROSPERITY DESCRIPTION: Leave a legacy that will imprint the world.

I love wearing stilettos—not just for snow spikes in the winter, but because they force me to walk tall and not slouchy and be proud of who I am. Even when I'm having a bad day, a pair of stilettos can honestly change that for me. Stilettos do make a mark on the world.

I often think of what mark I'm going to leave on this world—good or bad. I believe it's so important to have direction in that way when it comes to leaving a legacy. If we don't have clear intentions on what we want to leave behind, then how will we be able to leave the positive mark we want to leave in the world? Without clear intentions, our life becomes a kaleidoscope of disaster and "good intentions" left behind. A heart full of good intentions is procrastinating and truly leads to nowhere. So stop being full of "good intentions" and start taking action with intent!

One of my dreams in life is to do a TED Talk! So why not write it out for you? TED Talk or not, I do know exactly what I'd say for my five minutes of fame. (Oh, and by the way, this is my dream—my dream to create financial options for many generations to come and teach wealth stewardship!)

I never had any intention on selling life insurance. No eighteen-year-old ever dreams of being a life insurance salesperson. After college, at age twenty, I started in financial services.

At age twenty-one, I was presented with this idea from a life insurance wholesaler who was visiting our office that day. I don't actually remember who said it. I do remember where I was sitting in the office, and which way I was facing. I can see myself there listening to a guy who casually mentioned this idea that has become so important to me. I remember my brain began spinning with the idea.

Fundamentally, I want to help people create financial clarity and completely uncomplicate the financial industry, which I think is still very intimidating for many people. This is my passion—the deep down yearning in my stomach, the thing that gets me fired up without a doubt.

So given the way that I want to assist people, the idea that came to me that day was this: Every family, with proper financial planning and insurance in place, could be financially independent in less than four generations, or less than one hundred years. *Wow,* I thought. *This is huge!* And it is! This is my message, this is my *thing,* and this is my *why!*

Then it got me thinking, *Okay, how can this be true?* And then that led me to my next question: Why hasn't this happened yet, if it is as simple as that? (Remember, simple and easy are not the same thing!)

At that moment, the seed was planted, and it has been this thing nagging at me for over fifteen years now, nudging me in my moments of quietude....

Now I realize that behavioural psychology and natural human tendencies will make this idea virtually impossible on a large scale. Clearly, many families have made this a reality.

What would a world with well-managed resources look like? (Remember, all the abundance we will ever need is here already; we just haven't tapped into it.) It would have no starving people. It would have education available to everyone in abundance. It would have less cancer, less disease. It would have more full tummies and hopefully, in my dreams, more love. I know this is probably not going to happen in my lifetime, or maybe not ever. But after all, what is life without the aim to improve upon what we have already accomplished?

There is a way. Maybe just on paper; however, knowing the power of this is so important.

So I have set out to show you how families can be financially independent in less than four generations. That's my next book, by the way, and you are going to absolutely love it (What, did you honestly think I was going to give away my full TED Talk just yet?)

However, there is one thing that goes along with families creating lasting financial abundance and wealth, and that is finding your financial strength.

Here's my take on how to find your financial strength. I've discovered that it's not your net worth or how much money you have that determines your financial strength. I'm guessing that statement runs contrary to what most people believe in our society. As a financial professional, I view this much differently.

As Brené Brown suggests in her book *Daring Greatly*, our strength comes from vulnerability and believing that to be true—and I believe our financial strength comes from a place of vulnerability as well.

I think financial vulnerability is a balancing act between what we "know" and what we are able to admit that we "don't know" in regards to our financial situations. Finding that humble place in between is where perfectionism drowns alongside egos and shame dissipates. Clearly, this applies to more than just the financial areas of our lives. I think financial strength is finding the sweet spot where you can balance the living with the planning.

I've spent years in deep thought and mounds of education, floundering, seeking, failing, succeeding, figuring out my purpose, trying to find my place, figuring my whole life out, and then only to feel as though it's all been a useless waste of time and like I'm back at square one again—or that I maybe never left. This has been my quest. Truly, finding my financial strength within has been years in the making. As a self-loving recovering perfectionist, I've struggled like most to find my strength as a woman—including my financial strength. Although I'm nowhere near the top of this mountain, I also know now there is really no top to this mountain; it's more like a set of hills you travel up and down often.

So I share with you as a pro hill climber, and here are the five ways I am continuing to find and build my financial strength.

1. Hold On with Open Hands.

I think the big secret in life is to hold on with open hands; never hold anything tightly. This goes for people, investments, jobs, and relationships; anything we want to control. Live in a place where riches and blessings of all types are free to come and go from your life. If you can't leave this earth with it, then it's probably not yours anyway. Remember, it's hard to place a gift in a closed fist.

2. Plan Your Work, Work Your Plan—Then Let It Go.

Take action. Don't wait for someone else to tell you to do something. Don't forget to live in the ebb and flow of life—make your financial plans and work hard, yet be at peace with them not going your way. Be paradoxical in your mind, knowing you should make plans and set goals and work hard and that it's important in the moment, but also knowing that none of it means anything at the end of the day. You also need to be able to admit that you're right sometimes, you're wrong a lot, that you've succeeded and you've failed, and then move along.

3. Keep an Abundant Mindset.

A full 100 percent of our financial success has to do with our mindset. What we manifest financially comes from our mindset. Keep your financial mindset strong and positive. Abundance wants to flow to you. Keep reading positive books, blogs, and quotes. Keep writing down your goals, pen to paper (or in my case, whiteboard!). Surround yourself with the people you want to be like. In my practice, I know almost everything about my clients. I know not only the intimate details of their financial lives but also their health and well-being. Knowing so much about my clients, I see firsthand the deep connection between their health and financial well-being.

4. Love Your Money.

Take interest in and care for your money. Appreciate it. I'm not saying be greedy, or make it your god. I'm saying you need to be a good steward of the things you've been blessed with. Apathy breeds nothing. Who really wants to be around people who don't care or aren't interested in you? Money's no different. Treat your money good—seriously. Be thankful and grateful for every cent. Track it. You will manifest more of it. Care for your money, and it will care for you back.

5. Clear Your Money Blocks.

I know firsthand when I'm having a money block or money issue, it affects my mood, my attitude, my health, and my smile. I also know when I'm not feeling good, other areas of my life aren't doing so hot either, and the downward spiral begins. As you journey through life, you're always going to have money roadblocks in your way. The quicker you handle them is ultimately how you will be able to get the desired outcome you want sooner rather than later. Because when the money issues do arise (and they always will), they wreak havoc on all parts of your life, and this will show up in your physical health as mild depression, weight gain, fatigue, etc. Acknowledge your money block or issue, own it, declare it, clear it, free it, and let it go. If you give it no power, then it has none over your life.

So today, my fellow hill climbers (in stilettos—because women can do that!), I pour out a special blessing to you as you discover and continue building your financial strength within.

FUN SHOE FACT: High heels were originally made for men. It was a sign of virility, masculinity, and high status.

SOLE QUOTE: "Keep your heels, head, and standards high." —Coco Chanel

"Life is short; heels shouldn't be." —Brian Atwood

SOUL QUOTE: "Your life is made of two dates and a dash. Make the most of the dash." —Unknown

FAB READS:

➤ *The 4-Hour Work Week: Escape the 9-5, Live Anywhere, and Join the New Rich* by Timothy Ferriss

➤ *The Magic of Believing* by Claude M. Bristol

➤ *You Can if You Think You Can* by Norman Vincent Peale

SHOUT IT OUT: I have unlimited abundance in all areas of my life.

PUTTIN' ON THE SHOES:

➤ Answer these questions for yourself:
  · What do you want your legacy to be?
  · What do you want your legacy to look like? Physically?
  · What's your *why*?

➤ Once you have answered those questions in your journal, reengineer and start now!

SHOEBOX NOTES:

➤ There is no competition, no scarcity.

➤ Speak positively–minimize negative and scatological language, as it does you no favours!

➤ Love your money, and it will love you back.

STRUT TUNES:

➤ "We Danced Anyways" by Deana Carter

➤ "Follow Your Arrow" by Kacey Musgraves

➤ "Save the Last Dance" by Michael Bublé

➤ "Respect" by Aretha Franklin

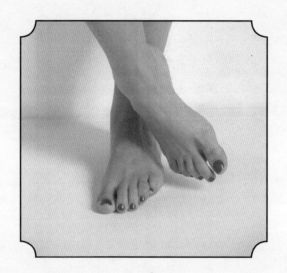

14

Barefoot

For it is better to die on your feet,
than to live on your knees.
—Emiliano Zapata

STYLE DESCRIPTION: Without shoes; feet that are bare.

PROSPERITY DESCRIPTION: You beautiful feet will move you in the direction you are heading.

Find your passion! It's so important, and it has *everything* to do with your financial health and physical well-being! As Marie Forleo, my favourite superstar on all things business for women, says, "No other person ever has, or ever will have, the unique blend of talents, strengths, and perspective that you have."[24] You are given desires for a reason, so follow them, because they are what you are passionate about. Then take that passion and shine it on the world. It is hard sometimes only because most of the world doesn't like bright lights, and when you make a commitment to *shine*, you need to shine and not care what others think or compare yourself to what others are doing. You will end up inspiring many others on your journey, and that is where impact is made on the world. So go for it; don't stand in the flip-flop of life, maybe just put on your tap shoes, and start tap-tap-tapping away. As someone wise once put it, "The secret to getting ahead is getting started" (source unknown).

So start. If you found your passion already, what's holding you back? What do dreams have to do with financial planning? *Everything.* What's the point of saving a dime if you haven't figured out how that dime is going to help fuel your dreams or your dreams as a family?

What good is a big pile of money sitting around with no dreams attached to it? Money loves definitive purpose. (FYI: people with big piles of money with no dreams attached to it end up investing in *other* people's dreams by default—what do you really think all this capital in our world is used for, anyways? People's ideas—people's dreams! You'll be lending out your capital for other's dreams until you finally figure out what yours are. Welcome to capitalism.)

The problem is most of us give lip service to our dreams, and most are too afraid to even dream a big dream at all. We (by we, I also mean myself) are too afraid to talk about it—afraid to fail, afraid to succeed. Afraid we will be alone, or no one will like us when

---

24 Marie Forleo, interview by Sherold Barr, "Interview with Marie Forleo: Founder of B-School," *Sherold Barr*, accessed April 6, 2016, http://sheroldbarr.com/interview-marie-forleo-founder-b-school/.

they see the real us. Afraid of what people will think. Afraid people won't love us.

Dreams push us right out of our comfort zone. They push us out of jobs we don't like or careers that pay us really well to stick around. They break down the walls we worked so hard to build up not to expose the real us; so often the shining part of us can stay hidden in those walls and die within. After all, that's what our society has tricked most of us into believing.

All retirement really is, is when people have made enough money, have enough money set aside, or have enough cash flow (e.g., pensions or government benefits) to quit their job and actually follow their dreams without the financial risk of putting it all on the line (and not everybody is in a position to do that). Retirees can finally follow their dreams in whatever shape or form they come in and take the financial consideration out of the equation altogether. I think as a whole we are turning to careers or jobs we actually love— if not right away, then soon after. No one sticks around in a job they don't like anymore, anyways. That would be ludicrous. However, I don't think that we have swung the pendulum quite the other way yet. I think there are lots of hidden dreams that have yet to bubble to the surface.

Everyone has dreams. Dreams make you an artist in something. You may be an actual artist, a business owner, a musician, a surgeon, a construction worker, a pilot, or gardener. Your dream is what fuels you. It's what makes you shine, and your eyes light up when you talk about it.

I'm a writer. (*Wow*! I don't think I have ever actually written those words before about myself!) I'm also a financial coach. And at 4:00 a.m. this morning, I'm doing what I love because I had an idea while I was sleeping, and I had to get it down immediately into Evernote. It literally got me out of bed, with no coffee! My blood is pumping. I'm excited to be here, in front of the fireplace, cozy and writing!

My mom is awesome. I was on the phone with her yesterday, and she told me she's heading to Phoenix next week to spend the next two and a half months playing her viola with an eighty-piece orchestra and a huge choir and make her art unfold into a beautiful

Christmas concert. I love my mom and the passion she has when she says she's going to do this. I can't wait to go see her play at Christmas. That is her dream. It is her art.

My Opa and Oma had a construction company and worked so hard, as immigrants do. I don't think it was their dream to build apartments, but they built them, rented them out, and that work afforded them their dream: a hobby farm, when they were around fifty years old. I remember growing up on that farm. I bet my grandparents worked harder at their chickens, sheep, tree farming, bee keeping, and vegetable garden than at construction. That second life was their dream, and my Opa Georg was famous in his little town, because everyone knew that that man was living his purpose, his passion; you could see it in his eyes, the way he talked, the way he loved everyone. Their money fuelled their dreams. It had purpose with passion, and it made a difference in that town and to our family—anyone in my family will tell you that.

I will tell you my story around following your dreams. The truth is, although I've known for years what my passion and dreams were, I finally married the two in my head. Dreams and passions are different elements and need to mutually meet for them to create magic!

What are your dreams?

Mine are financial coaching and writing and above all sharing this passion and knowledge with others, and somehow, in the last two years, my dream is starting to take shape, although my passion has always flustered below in my belly. I believe passion stirs deep within, while dreams whirl around us in a playful game, waiting to be caught.

Honestly, nothing is more fun to me than writing, sharing, or working because *I love my work*. I like it more than wake surfing or playing golf or wine tasting—and that is like cursing in my family.

This is how my dream happened for me: *true story*.

It was October 2012. I was driving home Friday afternoon from the Delta Lodge at Kananaskis in the Rocky Mountains after my work conference. The motivational speaker had struck a chord within me. I knew what I wanted to do with my life, but I actually didn't know what my specific dream was.

I was stuck.

I've known for many years I have something great to share with the world. But it was difficult to find my own voice in this jungle, with my own self-doubt yelling back at me, much louder than my own voice (and for those who know me know, I'm no shrinking violet—I'm loud!).

I remember driving down Highway 40, asking God to give me a sign. He literally responded with this. A sign I had seen many times before. A simple road sign.

"Lisa, what's holding you back?"

Somehow, that sign—that moment—changed my life (anytime God talks to you directly typically does!). I pondered that sign at so many crossroads in my life when the question needed to be asked, and I'm sure that sign will keep cropping up when I need it to.

So last Friday afternoon, October 9, 2015 (coincidentally, my daughter's eighth birthday), on my way home from the same convention out in Kananaskis, I saw the sign again. Actually, I asked to see the sign again. So I looked for it. And there it was. I pulled my car over, and, looking like a full-out tourist with my iPhone, I took a picture of this sign. It was my Thanksgiving blessing.

I finally knew my next step, because I finally know my destination—or at least what road I'm supposed to be on to get there. I've run out of excuses this year. Although fear will come along for the ride, I have nothing holding me back from my dreams, and I have a purpose to my financial plan. *I have nothing holding me back.* And it finally feels good to say that.

What's holding you back?

My message is to help amazing people create financial clarity and fund their dreams. My passion for women in relation to my passion for financial planning is exciting, and my dream is not only to change the lives of as many women as I can reach with my message, but it's also to change the lives of children. To do that, I hope to play a part and help solid financial education go into schools across Canada and into the world and help teach financial basics that I know aren't reaching a majority of our children. How great would it be if our children could teach our adults about financial responsibility? It may seem like a crazy, unreasonable thing that I am up to, and let me tell you it fuels me! So, with this book, I continue on with my journey and hope I can add value to your life in some small way. If I can do that, then I've accomplished a dream to share with you part of myself, in hopes that you get something from my sharing.

Also, I seriously want you to be part of this community! This is my life's purpose and passion, so I am requesting you to join me online or in person on this wonderful mission. My promise to you is that I will make every effort to help you, and if I don't know the answers, I will connect you with the resources or wonderful people who do and in turn, you can share your wealth of info with someone who has yet to discover some of this powerful information that will transform lives for the better and generations to come!

When my girls were learning which feet to put their shoes on, I would say, "You've put your shoes on the wrong feet!" Kids are amazing and don't really care, but then my sweet baby said to me, "But, Mama, those are the only feet I have!" No kidding, kid! You hit it bang on. Kids can say the wisest things sometimes. Those are the only feet you have! So I say, let's go through the shoe closet, try on some new shoes, get rid of some old shoes, make room for some new shoes, and find the shoes that make your feet want to run, dance the night away, step towards your dreams, and help you take the jump so you can fund your dreams and put your mark on this world.

This is your life, and I want you to *own* it. Are you willing to sign off on your work, the work of your life, and take full accountability for it? To be honest, there are so many areas of my life that I struggle to take ownership of. Health is one of them. If someone asked me to sign off on my health, the way an engineer would sign off on the building he designed for structural safety, I would not want to do it. It does not reflect my best work. My eating habits and exercise have massive room for improvement. Each of us has an area or two (or ten) that we need to work on. Believe it or not, finances are probably one of the easier ones to own!

No one can pee for you; there are some things you are going to have to do for yourself. (Although I guess a catheter does come in handy from time to time.)

Sometimes, life just gets to complicated. When I find myself in that place (which seems to be all the time!), I try to break down my life and reflect on the two questions below as my guide, and as part of my life's purpose.

I believe this is the simplest way of explaining the "how." *How* do we make a difference in every area and be the change we want to see in the world?

I also believe these are the only two things we need to ask ourselves in any situation in life to see whether we are on the right path, living in alignment with our purpose, and discovering the secret to living an extraordinary life. Ask yourself these two questions all the time, as much as possible:

1 Is this out of love? (Is what I'm doing or saying or sharing coming from a place of love?)

2 How can I serve? How can I be of help right now in my situation? What can I do to help or to be of service in some way? How can I add value?

These are the two questions I've discovered that really shaped my life. And, yes, they are evergreen questions, questions that we should ask ourselves in every conversation and write them on our hearts, in our minds, and in the sky.

These two questions are for our relationships, our family, our friends, our lover, our partner, our business, our work, our jobs, and our transactions. They are meant to keep you in alignment in every area of your life by allowing you to do a quick head and heart check.

What would the world look like if everybody asked these two questions of themselves and were able to be authentic in their answers and their sharing?

One verse that keeps coming to mind is, "Blessed are the feet that bring the good news" (Romans 10:15). In whatever your journey, whatever your path, whatever your walk in life, I challenge you to have beautiful feet—feet that carry you to fulfill your purpose while you walk this earthly sphere. As you walk through your life, don't forget to love on your feet. And when you take a step, take it confidently. When you make a financial decision, make it confidently. Remember, people are people. We all make mistakes, and what matters most is what we learn from them. And I'll say it again: sometimes we have to stumble forward. Okay, so I didn't call this book *Stumbling Forward*, for various reasons, first being that

Strut

I probably wouldn't be able to give it away. I did however call this book *Strut*.

And with that, I commission you to go out into the world and show off your feet, with your footwear of choice. Be proud of who you are, love all the people in your life and who cross your path daily, and find the hidden pleasure in all things. And don't be too hard on yourself, for we are usually our biggest critics. So when you make a bad financial decision, or in any area of your life, learn from it, and don't be hard on yourself for it. Just keep on keeping on, stand tall and proud, and *you will strut.*

SOLE QUOTE: "It's great to be known for your shoes, but it's better to be known for your sole." —Kenneth Cole

SOUL QUOTE: "Forget not that the earth delights to feel your bare feet and the winds long to play with your hair." —Kahlil Gibran

"I would rather walk barefoot than wear the shoes of mediocrity." —Lisa Elle

FAB READS:

- The Holy Bible (Proverbs is a good place to start for wisdom, and it's still the world's best-selling book!)

- *The War of Art: Break Through the Blocks and Win Your Inner Creative Battles* by Steven Pressfield

- *Big Magic: Creative Living Beyond Fear* by Elizabeth Gilbert

SHOUT IT OUT: I am blessed, full of love and gratitude.

Lisa Elle

PUTTIN' ON THE SHOES:

🥿 Pour out *you*!

🥿 Find *your true* message, and then pour that out on others.

SHOEBOX NOTES:

🥿 Own it!

🥿 Be in alignment with yourself.

🥿 Tips to *a successful life*:

In every moment ask yourself, "Is this out of *love*? And how can I serve? How can I help in this situation?" I think if you can do that, you will more likely be dramatically successful in your life, and in your impact on humanity.

STRUT TUNES:

🥿 "I've Got the Music in Me" by Thelma Houston

🥿 "Always Sing" by Raelynn

🥿 "Perfect" by Martina McBride

🥿 "Emmanuel" by Chris Botti (My favourite instrumental song of all time!)

I have taken all of the "Shout It Out" affirmations and complied them into one positive, powerful statement for you to read, write, profess, pray, speak, share, and shout in affirmation.

I am amazing. I create my life.

I forgive myself.

I am free.

I am *strong*.

I live the life I was called to live.

I love myself.

I love others unconditionally.

I have all the knowledge of the
universe available to me.

I teach and share with others.

I am a good steward over the money
and resources placed in my care.

Resources and money flow easily to me.

My abundance is constantly increasing.

I have unlimited abundance
in all areas of my life.

I am blessed, full of love and gratitude.

WANNA STRUT WITH ME?

Check out my 6-Week Money Makeover
Online Course and Community.

Click here to get Module 0 for free
and get the Miracle Money Map Template.
www.ellementsgroup.com

ACKNOWLEDGMENTS

I'd like to thank the following people from the bottom of my heart:

MOM AND DAD: your love and support mean so much to me. A big thank you to my dad, who once took his eighteen-year-old daughter to an investor's course on how to trade stocks and options—which no doubt sparked my entire career and love for the financial industry—and for the financial boardroom meeting and drivers contract you made for me and caring enough to do that. Mom, thank you for just loving the un-perfect me, no matter what! *Thank you!* Also, thank you to Bunny and Joe, my awesome in-laws!

MY SHOES EN BLANC GIRLS: thank you for coming out on September 28, 2014, and supporting this book I was writing. That day was such an encouragement to me! Thank you to some of the most important women in my life: Margaret Loewen (my mama), Natalie Fuglestveit (my sis), Paula Loewen (my sis), Wanda Klapstein, Carrie Spring, Jennifer Klapstein, Vanessa Hagen, Ashley Ruud, Andrea Proude, Michelle Klapstein, Vaneesa Cline, Ingrid Cividino, Rummy Rendina, Janice Piet, Heather Alvas, Andrea Bye, Maddie Moss, April Schroeder, Brittney Caouette, Sharla Barsi, Colleen Loewen, and Tara Hopkins. You ladies are so strong, and I feel your power and support every day. I am blessed you women are part of my walk.

MY AMAZING TEAM THAT HAS WORKED WITH ME TO HELP KICK MY BUTT TO GET HERE: Pam Tennant, you truly are a huge asset to my business, and in sharing my vision. Your smile while we work every day is a blessing, and your faith has propelled me forward. Tamara Schroeder, for all your help and support with editing. Christine Lumgair, thank you for making me shine this book out to the world and not leave it in my basement collecting dust!

MY ONLINE SUPPORT GROUPS OF WOMEN ENTREPRENEURS WHO INSPIRE ME DAILY: Kat Loterzo for pushing my butt daily, my Landmark community, Brooke Castillo, Marie Forleo and Team and my B-Schooler's, and even though I may never meet most of my awesome online gals, you all speak into my life, and we are still connected in a unique way, and so important to have these communities connecting women online and support!

MY FRIENDS WHO BELIEVED IN ME: when I had my breakdowns and felt the whole world was against me, you talked me off the ledge, encouraged me, and breathed life into me at times when my emotions totally took over and ran the show. Thank you! Also, a special thank you to D – thank you for cheering me on and for being a financial sounding board.

MY SHOPPING CLUB GIRLS (JUGS): you kept me sane every month by letting me get the crazy out! You make Cochrane the greatest place to live, and I value our time and friendship more than you know. We may have to work on our table dancing routine.

MY AMAZING BROKERAGES: you have stood behind me for over twelve years, and you truly support and fight for the independent advisors across Canada. I'm truly grateful for you and all the work you do in our industry!

I AM THANKFUL FOR MY GRANDMA MIMI , who encouraged me to write a book many years ago and inspired me by writing and publishing the story of her life. To my Oma, the matriarch of our family, who is one of the strongest women I know, and all your advice and love is evident by our growing fun, loving, crazy family. To my extended family spread out across Canada (Schedlers, Loewens, Lindsays and Lyttles), I'm thankful that we came from good roots! What a blessing, and I thank you for your support in my life and this book as well!

Strut

MY JOE: you gave me space to write, and you didn't quit. Watching your love for our daughters is one of my greatest blessings and joys. Thank you for being you. I love this crazy journey we are on! With your love and support, I am truly blessed by having you in my life. I will always love you!

MY SWEET D'S: I love you to the moon and back! Thank you for being you and teaching me so much about myself as I went on that crazy journey of parenthood. I'm so blessed that God chose me to be the mama to two beautiful and amazing girls.

BIBLIOGRAPHY

Arylo, Christina, quoted in Tiny Buddha: Simple Wisdom for Complex Lives. Accessed January 16, 2016, http://tinybuddha.com/wisdom-author/christine-arylo/.

Banerjee, Preet. "Why 2.5 Billion Heartbeats Might Change the Way You Think About Money." TED Talk. *TEDxUTSC.* February 12, 2013, http://tedxtalks. ted.com/video/Why-2-5-billion-heartbeats-migh.

Brait, Ellen. "Inside the $1m Hunt to Bring Dorothy's Stolen Ruby Slippers Home." *The Guardian* (July 14, 2015). Accessed January 16, 2016, http://www.theguardian.com/film/2015/jul/14/ wizard-of-oz-dorothy-stolen-ruby-slippers-1m-reward.

Choron, Harry, and Sandy Choron. *Money: Everything You Never Knew About Your Favourite Thing to Find, Covet, Save and Spend* (San Francisco: Chronicle Books, 2011).

Clason, George S. *The Richest Man in Babylon* (Lulu.com, 2013).

Coreen T. Sol. *Practically Investing: Smart Investment Techniques Your Neighbour Doesn't Know About* (Bloomington, IN: iUniverse, 2014).

Covey, Stephen. *The Seven Habits of Highly Successful People: Restoring the Character Ethic* (New York: Simon and Schuster, 1989).

Duckworth, Angela Lee. "The Key to Success? Grit." TED Talk. *Ted Talks Education.* April, 2013, https://www.ted.com/talks/ angela_lee_duckworth_the_key_to_success_grit?language=en.

Forleo, Marie. Interview by Sherold Barr, "Interview with Marie Forleo: Founder of B-School." *Sherold Barr.* Accessed April 6, 2016, http://sheroldbarr.com/ interview-marie-forleo-founder-b-school/.

———. "When Inspiration Backfires." *Readable.* Accessed April 6, 2016, http://www.allreadable.com/e22a5LY6.

"Great Journeys Canvas." Curly Girl Design. Accessed January 16, 2016, http://www.curlygirldesign.com/shop/home-and-office/great-journeys-canvas/.

Hill, Napoleon. *Read, Think and Grow Rich: All Time Bestseller Reproduced and Updated for the 21st Century*, ed.Veli-Matti Vesikko (public domain, 2016).

Huffington, Arianna. *Thrive: The Third Metric to Redefining Success and Creating a Life of Well-Being, Wisdom, and Wonder.* New York: Harmony Books. 2014.

Lammam, Charles, and Milagros Palacios. "How Much Taxes Do Canadians Really Pay?" *Troy Media.* April 27, 2012, http://www.troymedia.com/2012/04/27/how-much-tax-do-canadians-really-pay/.

"Lottery Winner Statistics." Statistic Brain. *Camelot Group PLC.* Accessed January 16, 2016, http://www.statisticbrain.com/lottery-winner-statistics/.

Maxwell, John C. *25 Ways to Win People: How to Make Others Feel Like a Million Bucks* (Nashville, TN: Nelson Publishers, 2005).

Murray, Nick. "Client's Corner: It's Always About Time, Never About Timing." *Financially Sound Life Planning.* Accessed January 16, 2016, http://financiallysound.ca/wp-content/uploads/2014/03/s-Always-about-Time-not-Timing.pdf.

———. *Serious Money: The Art of Marketing Mutual Funds* (Shrewsbury, NJ: R.A. Stanger, 1991).

Nightingale, Earl. "20 Minutes that Can Change Your Life." YouTube video. 18:49. Posted by MartyMcFly1985. August 12, 2013, https://www.youtube.com/watch?v=gYQejJmKbx8.

Ponder, Catherine. *The Dynamic Laws of Prosperity*, rev. ed. (Marina del Rey, CA: DeVorss, 1985).

Roberts, Russ, quoted in Yaron Brook and Don Watkins. "When It Comes to Wealth Creation, there Is No Pie." *Forbes* (June 14, 2011).

"Shoes History—Facts and History of Shoes." *Shoe History and Facts.* Accessed January 16, 2016, http://www.shoeshistoryfacts.com/.

Sinek, Simon "Start with Why," TED Talk. *TEDx Puget Sound.* September 2009, https://www.ted.com/talks/simon_sinek_how_great_leaders_inspire_action?language=en.

Socrates, quoted in Plato, *Apology*, trans. Benjamin Jowett. *The Internet Classics Archive*, Massachusetts Institute of Technology, http://classics.mit.edu/Plato/apology.html.

Lisa Elle

"Tim Minchin UWA Address 2013." YouTube video, 18:16. Posted by The University of Western Australia. October 7, 2013, https://www.youtube.com/watch?v=yoEezZD71sc.

Vanderkam, Laura. *What the Most Successful People Do Before Breakfast: And Two Other Short Guides to Achieving More at Work and at Home* (New York: Portfolio, 2013).

#8q7o5r5k<3